SOLDIER WITHOUT A GUN

Life as a Conscientious Objector

JAN PARKINSON

Lilly,

I hope the time you spend
with my book will be as
meaningful and rewarding for
you as writing it has been for me.

For Jayne,

the remarkable woman

who buttons my buttons

and fills my days with love.

ISBN (Softcover): 978-1-09839-638-1
ISBN (eBook): 978-1-09839-639-8

ONE
The Good Guys

I t was a simpler time.

Or it certainly seemed like one.

The country was brimming with confidence in the 1950s. World War II was over, and to hear some tell it, we had defeated the Germans, the Japanese, and the Italians virtually single-handedly.

We had shown we were the good guys, and since there were no other takers, the U.S. assumed the role of leader of the free world.

The GI Bill was sending veterans to college and helping them buy homes in new bedroom communities that were springing up around cities all across the country. The unemployment rate was low. There was pent-up demand for all sorts of products that had been scarce or rationed during the war.

People were talking about "the American dream" as if it was a divine right. And why not? We had earned a little peace and prosperity, hadn't we?

Growing up as a White kid in a brand-new suburb outside a Midwestern city, I was a recipient of this largesse.

So it was perfectly natural that Hopalong Cassidy was my first hero.

In Hoppy's world, you were either a good guy or a bad guy, and he was the quintessential good guy, except unlike other classic good guys of the 1940s and 1950s, he wore a black hat, black pants, and a black shirt. He had a pair of pearl-handled six-shooters and was not afraid to use them. When a bad guy was sneaking up on him from behind, he could quickly turn, draw his weapons, and shoot the gun out of the villain's hand without taking time to aim. In a showdown, Hoppy would sometimes shoot the bad guy, but he only resorted to violence when it was absolutely necessary to protect "decent folks"— such as the old-maid school marm, the farmer's widow, or the saloon girl with the heart of gold.

In his era, Hollywood heroes like Hopalong Cassidy were not complicated characters. They were not conflicted or flawed. They were pure of heart and good guys through and through.

The bad guys were just as one-dimensional. Evil to the core. There was never any doubt that they would get their comeuppance at the hands of the good guys like Hoppy before the credits rolled.

I was six years old when I discovered Hopalong Cassidy. He helped shape my early view of the world, especially the concept of the legitimate use of violence. At that time, American troops were involved in an undeclared war that was euphemistically called the Korean Conflict. I was only vaguely aware that we were in another war because of the way my parents talked about it. When their friends came to our house for dinner or a game of bridge, their voices rarely rose above a whisper if Korea was mentioned. "We don't want to alarm the kids" they would explain.

I had no idea who we were fighting or why. Despite that, I knew for certain that we were the good guys because...well, we just always were the good guys.

In those days, kids did not interrupt adult conversations, but the solution to their worries about Korea seemed obvious to me. So, one night when we had company at our house for dinner, I finally spoke up:

"Why don't they just send Hopalong Cassidy to Korea?" I said. "He could take care of the enemy."

There was a long, uneasy silence, followed by some barely suppressed laughter. Every kid knows what that means: I was being innocent and adorable—the ultimate putdown from an adult. I didn't know what was wrong with my idea, but it was very clear that it had been rejected by the adult world.

Despite the adults' rejection, Hopalong Cassidy's influence was still readily apparent in my daily play.

Growing up in the 1950s, I played "army" with the other boys in my neighborhood. (We didn't play cowboys and Indians because nobody would ever have agreed to be an Indian in those days.)

While we did not have the sophisticated plastic assault rifle replicas that are available today, that did not stop us from killing one another. Most of us had cap pistols—six-shooter revolvers just like Hoppy's (or so we liked to pretend). It was rare for any of us to actually have a roll of caps. When we did, it allowed us to fire off fifty rounds without reloading our six-shooters, just like the heroes of Western movies. The rest of the time, we simply made the sound of gunfire. I was an expert at making the "ricochet" sound.

When I wanted more firepower, I used a croquet mallet as my Thompson submachine gun and made the rapid-fire sound effect as I sprayed bullets on the enemy.

Sometimes we wandered into the wooded area across the street from my house searching out imaginary enemies and mowing them down.

Other times, the group split into sides, but that always led to arguments.

We could never agree on who got to be the good guys—the Americans. Eventually, that decision was tabled so that we would have enough time to kill each other before our mothers called us home for dinner.

Even more hotly contested was the question of whether or not you had "been hit." When someone pointed a six-shooter at you—or the barrel of a croquet mallet—and made the appropriate sound of a gun being fired, it was customary to duck or jump aside and shout, "You missed me!"

The debate that ensued would often consume much of the remaining playing time and was rarely resolved.

My younger brother was the exception. His specialty was dying in some sort of dramatic fashion. He would stumble around clutching his chest and moaning, eventually fall to the ground, and breathe his last. He was especially fond of dying on top of a hill so he could roll all the way to the bottom. He once died falling out of a tree. But his most dramatic death was when he was shot while standing on the seat of his tricycle. He was coming down the street, bent over holding the handlebars. As he turned sharply into our driveway, he was shot. His "jeep" overturned, and he was thrown into the yard where he expired with a mournful groan. My brother's devotion to the art of dying meant he always had a few cuts, bruises, or skinned knees. Of all the neighborhood kids, my little brother was the one who looked the most like he might actually have been to war.

When we tired of the battle, we would gather on our back porch for Kool-Aid and an analysis of the day's activities. Usually we simply continued the arguments about who had been shot. In the end, however, we all lived to fight another day.

When there was no one around to play army, I would get out my army set—an assortment of those green molded plastic soldiers that appeared more recently in the *Toy Story* movies. They made it possible to play army by myself. And, of course, I got to decide who had been shot and who had been missed. I liked the soldiers who were flat on their stomachs, aiming a Browning Automatic Rifle at the enemy. They were smart. Staying low to the ground, they were not giving their enemy much of a target.

There was a serious side to playing army, whether it was with the little green men or my neighborhood friends. The game shaped my attitude about the use of violence. Clearly, I had a child's view of war. The adults saw that when I suggested that we send Hopalong Cassidy to Korea. My wars were just games. At the end of the day, I went home and regardless of how many times I had been killed, I knew I would be ready for more the next day.

What I learned from Hoppy and experienced in our war games was reinforced in elementary school.

The American history that we were taught in those early grades made it clear we were the good guys. We went to war with the best possible motives—to save the school marms of the world and to protect our way of life. But we did so reluctantly, and our cause was always just. On the other hand, our enemies—usually the Japs or the Commies—were always evil.

According to our history books, America was a country that was "discovered" by White Christian males from Western Europe. They were fleeing oppression. They were seeking freedom and what they felt were certain inalienable rights.

And, in turn, they "tamed the West," subdued the savages, and kidnapped citizens of Africa to provide an agricultural workforce in the South.

Growing up, I could not see that view was not only naïve but also arrogant. Perhaps unwittingly so, but arrogant nonetheless.

And the adults were blind to that too, or at least pretended to be.

TWO

The Plan

In the fall of 1967, I enlisted in the United States Army. It was not a carefully reasoned decision. In fact, it was barely a decision at all. I had already received a draft notice from the local Selective Service Board when I signed the papers that would make me a real soldier. One way or another, I was going to be in the Army.

However, in June 1966, just over a year earlier, my world was a vastly different place. I could see my future stretching out in front of me as clear and straight as a western Kansas highway, and the United States Army was nowhere in sight.

I had just graduated from college and was excited about starting my first "real job" as an advertising and promotion copywriter for Hallmark Cards, a creative job with a creative company that was in a period of rapid growth.

My wife, Ami, and I were expecting our first child, an event we hoped would be welcomed more enthusiastically by our parents than our marriage had been. We found an inexpensive but very roomy apartment in the Westport area of Kansas City, a neighborhood that was beginning to be rediscovered by young adults.

The economy was strong, not yet showing signs of the mini-recession that would follow a few years later. Jobs were plentiful for new college grads, and we were all feeling optimistic about our futures despite the growing war in Vietnam and the dissent it was creating in the U.S.

In two years, the war had moved from the back pages of the newspaper to page one. American involvement had escalated rapidly with the number of U.S. troops on the ground jumping from 23,000 in 1964 to 385,000 by the end of 1966. To meet the need for fresh troops, the monthly draft totals had grown from 10,000 to 30,000. Opposition to the war was growing too. Anti-war protests were occurring on several college campuses and in many large cities. But separated by 8,000 miles, Vietnam was still as far away in most people's awareness as it was in actual distance.

It sounds incredibly naïve to say this now, but I never expected Vietnam to directly impact my life. I didn't know anyone who was in Vietnam. In fact, I didn't know anyone in any branch of the service except for a couple of older fraternity brothers who had been in the Navy ROTC program in college at the University of Kansas. Ami's father had been a career Army man, but since he died of a heart attack before Ami and I were engaged, I didn't really know him.

I had never been especially concerned about the draft. My student deferment had kept me off of the draft board's "eligible for military service" list for my four years of college. With a child on the way, I was reclassified III-A, which at the time was even safer than my II-A classification as a student.

Monday, June 13, 1966, was my first day at Hallmark. The job was a good fit right from the start. Although I was the youngest and least experienced of the twenty or so artists and writers in the department, my boss had been impressed with my portfolio of work from college and thought I had a fresh perspective, so he often steered the most interesting and challenging projects my way. I was already imagining myself moving rapidly up the management ladder.

Four weeks later, on July 10, a lazy Sunday morning, Ami's water broke, and she started having contractions. I called the doctor, my parents, and Ami's mother. My parents decided to come to the hospital and join me as I waited. Ami's mother told me to call her back when I had some news.

I grabbed the bag that had been sitting by the door for the past three weeks, and we headed for the hospital.

Over the next fifteen hours, Butterfly McQueen's line from *Gone with the Wind* kept coming back to me: "I don't know nothin' about birthin' babies."

Why was it taking so long? Why does it seem like everyone is moving in slow motion? And where the hell is the doctor?

Finally, sometime after 2:00 a.m. on Monday, July 11, our son, Rory Michael, was born. He was complete. All the parts were there, and they were working the way they were supposed to.

Mother and baby spent two nights in the hospital, and on Wednesday morning, we brought him home and placed him in the antique cradle my mother had given us.

The two of us just sat and watched Rory sleeping peacefully. In the miracle of the moment, we felt like a family.

Over the next few weeks, the pages of our pristine copy of Dr. Spock took on a well-used look. At times, Rory would start crying for no discernable reason. We changed his diaper, fed him, tried marathon sessions in the rocking chair, offered a pacifier, and when all that failed, we would get in the car and drive around the block a few times. It always worked. He quickly fell asleep and would stay asleep...until he was placed back in his cradle. When I asked the doctor about it, he said "Babies cry. Just try to relax."

Overall, Rory was a happy, good-natured baby, and I would often find myself returning to watch him in total amazement as he slept.

We took him to visit his grandparents and to a nearby park where the three of us would lie on a blanket in the sun. My father began finding reasons to drop in on his way home from work. We took pictures. We sang, read, and talked to him. We imagined him growing up.

One weekend in early September, my friend David came for a visit before heading off to Harvard Law School. We were delighted to show him this marvelous creature we had created. He seemed impressed—or at least acted like it. But on Sunday afternoon, Rory started fussing. He couldn't seem to get comfortable and cried for long stretches. Nothing seemed to calm him down. Overnight, he developed a fever and diarrhea.

After David left on Monday morning, we took Rory to the pediatrician. Although he did not offer a diagnosis or even speculate about what was wrong, he was clearly concerned. He told us to take

Rory to the hospital where he would undergo some tests. The doctor would come by later in the day.

When we got to the hospital, Rory was placed in isolation. His was the only crib in a room big enough for six. The crib was covered with an oxygen tent.

He looked so small…and alone.

There is a strange transformation that occurs when you spend long hours with a loved one in a hospital. You become detached from whatever is going on in the rest of the world. It no longer seems real. The hospital becomes your world. And our world was a cold, dark, nearly empty room.

When the doctor came by at the end of that first day, he tried to be reassuring but acknowledged the serious nature of this unidentified ailment. There was nothing definitive the next morning, but the doctor said meningitis was a possibility. That was like a punch in the gut. I didn't really know anything about the disease, but I knew enough to be scared.

"Maybe we'll know more this afternoon," he said hopefully.

Over the next several hours, I repeated a silent prayer: "Please, God, don't let it be meningitis."

My prayer was answered but not the way I wanted. That afternoon the doctor told us that Rory had leukemia. He was going to die. In a baby, whose body was growing rapidly, the leukemia would take over rapidly too. He would be gone in a matter of hours…a day or two at the most.

We called our parents and Father Hingston, our Episcopal priest, who came to the hospital to be with us.

Our priest suggested Rory be baptized. With all the turmoil of the past few days, it had not occurred to us, but of course, we agreed. Father Hingston asked a nurse for something to put water in, and she returned with a beat-up aluminum saucepan. She apologized. It was all she could find she said. But somehow it seemed more appropriate to me than a beautiful polished silver container.

On Wednesday morning, we were alone in the room when a nurse walked in, looked at Rory, and called a "Code Blue." In what seemed like seconds, half a dozen people came rushing into the room followed by a "crash cart." We were ushered into the hall and watched through a window as the medical team crowded around the bed.

Of course, there was nothing for them to do. After a few minutes, they began to slowly shuffle out of the room. Our doctor came across the street from his office to tell us that Rory was gone. Our son had been with us for only sixty-four days, and yet he had made a difference in our lives simply by being born and again when he died.

I don't remember much of what happened next. I know someone from the hospital gave us some papers and told us what we needed to do.

Eventually, we were alone in the hall, and the hospital slipped back into its rhythm.

We walked outside. The sidewalks seemed to be full of people who were enjoying a beautiful fall day. A couple holding hands. A group of boisterous kids. Smiles and laughter. It didn't seem real.

"How can this be?" I thought. "Don't they know what just happened inside those doors? How can the world just go on as if nothing had changed?"

But I knew the world would go on.

And even though my world had changed, I knew that somehow it would go on too.

In the weeks that followed, our apartment became a sad, quiet place. Although Rory's death dominated our lives, we could not bring ourselves to talk about it. I think we both knew that we should, but neither of us wanted to be the one to bring it up. To say it out loud would be too painful.

Work became my refuge. There were other people, other things to do, other things to talk about…distractions from the reminders that filled our apartment.

Ami, however, was no longer a mother and seemed unable to find a new purpose.

She decided she wanted to get a job, so I talked to someone in Hallmark's personnel department, and he arranged for her to work as a salesperson in the folk art/decorative accessories department of the upscale, Hallmark-owned Hall's department store in downtown Kansas City.

While work was a form of escape for me, it was not for Ami. She took her sadness to work with her. She hated the job. After a couple of unhappy months for her and her manager, she was let go.

She made clothes. She cooked. She talked about going back to school and started investigating nursing programs.

Around the first of the year, a form letter from my local draft board showed up in our mailbox. It was time to update the information in my file. That's when it hit me: Rory's death would be the end of my III-A classification. I was going to jump to the top of the "eligible for military service" list.

I filled out the forms informing them of Rory's death and sent them back to my draft board.

My world was about to fall apart again.

THREE
Everything Changes

A nother letter from Selective Service Board Number 33 appeared in our mailbox before long. As expected, I had been reclassified I-A: "available for military service." The letter also informed me that I could expect to receive a draft notice in the near future.

But one night when I came home from work, Ami was all smiles. She was pregnant again.

We breathed a sigh of relief. I notified the draft board, and my III-A classification was restored. We could get our lives back.

But fate wasn't having any part of it. Near the end of the first trimester, Ami miscarried. Her doctor warned that another pregnancy right away could be dangerous. He also suggested she start seeing a therapist, which she did.

I let the draft board know about the miscarriage knowing the information would trigger another reclassification most likely followed by a draft notice. I was worried about leaving Ami in her current state of mind. The death of her first baby followed by a miscarriage and an unfulfilling job left her struggling with depression.

When I received my next reclassification letter, I decided to try a different approach: "registrant deferred by reason of extreme hardship to dependents." If the draft board agreed, my III-A would be restored. I knew it was a long shot, but I wrote to the draft board explaining our situation and enclosed a short and somewhat vague note from the psychiatrist she had started seeing.

My status was put on hold while the draft board considered this new information, and I used the time to explore my options.

That didn't take long because there really weren't any. The Navy, Air Force, and every reserve unit was easily meeting their quotas, and the National Guard had a waiting list of applicants. The Marines were still looking for "a few good men," and the Army was looking for warm bodies.

I just couldn't picture myself as a Marine, so that's how I found myself shaking hands with Sergeant First Class Stead at the Armed Forces Examining and Entrance Station on Pershing Road a few blocks from Hallmark.

If you were going to build the ideal Army recruiter from scratch, you would end up with a Sgt. First Class Stead. He was an impressive figure—tall and blonde with the rugged good looks of an all-American football player. He knew his role and played it well. He was obviously an adherent of the well-known adage: "The secret of success is sincerity. Once you can fake that, you've got it made."

I needed someone to listen to my story, give me an honest appraisal of my options, and toss in a little reassurance. And it just so happened that Sgt. Stead was having a special on "honest appraisals" that very day.

He advised me not to wait for a draft notice. He said if I enlisted, I could opt for delayed entry, which would give me ninety days to make sure my wife's situation and other details were taken care of. He also urged me to consider Officer Candidate School (OCS). As a college graduate, I would likely qualify for OCS, and he assured me that even though it would add eight months to my enlistment, life in the Army as an officer was vastly superior to that of a draftee. But he cautioned me that once I had received a draft notice, none of that would be possible.

He suggested that I go ahead and fill out all the paperwork but not sign it yet. That way if and when I was reclassified, everything would be in place, and I could just come in and sign the papers. Everything he said seemed to make sense, so I left the recruiting office with a stack of forms to fill out, a bunch of recruiting pamphlets, and a slick color brochure about OCS. I also had an appointment to return in two weeks to take the written tests and physical exam.

The recruiting materials were full of vague hyperbole—the "be all that you can be" stuff—and therefore of little interest to me. The OCS brochure, however, was another matter. It was extremely well-planned and executed. I had never considered the possibility of becoming an Army officer, so I poured over every word of the copy and examined every photograph to see what I could learn.

The brochure painted a very positive picture of life as a U.S. Army officer, but much of it was focused on the résumé value *after* leaving the Army. The copy boasted that the leadership training and experience gained as an Army officer would be highly desirable among senior executives in major civilian corporations.

But one sentence in the brochure interrupted this idyllic view of an officer's career. It leaped off the page when I first read it: *An officer's primary responsibility is the management of violence.*

My initial thought was that I had misread it. I reread it several times, but the words were right there on the page in black and white. I had read it correctly, but I couldn't understand why the Army chose to stress the violent aspect of an officer's job description.

It was just nine words. Of all that Sgt. First Class Stead had told me and every word that I read in the materials he provided, what I remembered most vividly was: *An officer's primary responsibility is the management of violence.*

The words haunted me as I faced a future that I was virtually certain would include military service…and those words would eventually change my life again.

FOUR

The First Test

A few days before I was due to return for qualifying tests and my physical exam, I received a reminder in the mail from Sgt. First Class Stead. When I showed up at the Armed Forces Examining and Entrance Station, he was waiting for me.

"Oh, good," he said, visibly relieved. "You're here."

A rather strange greeting, I thought. Of course, it really wasn't me he was worried about. I represented a checkmark against his monthly quota. Perhaps two if I qualified for OCS.

The cynical part of my brain was thinking, "I probably could have asked him to pick me up. And had him bring me a coffee... and a donut."

However there was no time for idle speculation as he directed me to the exam room, a brightly lit space with all the ambience and charm of a prison. The room was packed—twenty or thirty guys sitting at high-school-style desks.

I don't remember many details about the tests. I think there were three or four. The first was the basic qualifying test that everyone had to take. As best as I can recall, it was a multiple-choice test with about one hundred questions. The one thing I can say for certain is that it was the easiest exam I have ever taken. I finished it quickly and had checked my answers when Sgt. First Class Stead noticed I was sitting looking off into space. Well, looking at the gray concrete block walls actually.

He came over and whispered, "Is everything OK?"

"I'm finished," I said.

"Why don't you check your answers, just in case?" he suggested.

"I did," I said. "Twice."

I don't think he believed me, but he took my answer sheet to another sergeant seated at a table at the front of the room who started grading it.

There was nothing for me to do except sit and wait for the others in the room to finish.

A few minutes later, another recruiter came up to the young kid sitting next to me and set his test paper on the desk in front of him.

"I have marked a few questions that you might want to think about a little longer," he said. He gave the kid a little smile and walked away.

The kid just sat there for a moment. He looked confused.

"He's telling you which ones you got wrong," I whispered.

It took a few seconds for the light to go on, but he finally started through the test again.

I never found out how he did, but I'm guessing he eventually passed. I don't think the recruiter's actions did the kid any real favors. He didn't do the Army any favors either. But he had protected the checkmark on his quota scorecard for that day.

There was a psychological profile test we had to take and perhaps a third exam, but the final written test of the day for me was an aptitude test for OCS. It was bizarre.

Each question offered a choice between two activities, scenarios, or skills. You had to pick the answer that was the most appropriate for you. That's a standard testing approach, but in this test, the options seemed far too obvious. I can only recall one of the actual examples from that test: "I would rather: Read a book OR Lead a group of men in marching."

Assuming that you were taking the test because you wanted to get into OCS, which answer would you pick?

The answers seemed so blatantly obvious, I thought at least some of them must be trick questions, so I went through the entire test several times carefully looking for hidden trickery but finding none.

At the end of the day, Sgt. First Class Stead tracked me down again and let me know that I had passed with flying colors. In fact, he said, it was the first time he had ever had one of his recruits get all of the answers right on the basic qualifying test. I didn't really believe that, but I was willing to accept the compliment anyway.

The day was over and I went home, but a future that included the Army now seemed closer than ever.

FIVE

You're in the Army Now

I didn't have to wait very long.

I wasn't surprised when the draft board turned down my "extreme hardship to dependents" appeal. Their letter was short and to the point: I had not presented sufficient information to support a claim of extreme hardship, but if I had additional information to offer, they would reconsider my status. If not, I could expect to hear from them (i.e., receive a draft notice) within four to six weeks.

My induction notice was in my mailbox two weeks later. It was Wednesday, October 25, 1967.

In a panic, I called Sgt. First Class Stead.

He was annoyed, but not alarmed. Obviously he had been down this road before, and he was not about to let an enlistee slip away from him at the last minute.

"We are not having this conversation," he said. "Come in first thing tomorrow morning. Can you be here by 9:00 a.m.? Don't have anything you've received from the draft board with you except your draft card. I don't know about any communication you've had with them, so don't say anything about the draft board to anyone while you are here. And one last thing: your induction notice won't arrive until Friday."

"If you say so," I said.

"No," he said sharply. "You say so."

I was at the Armed Forces Examining and Entrance Station shortly before 9:00 a.m., and Sgt. First Class Stead was waiting with the forms I needed to sign. It only took a few minutes. Sgt. First Class Stead extended his right hand, and we exchanged a quick shake, but our thoughts were in two different places.

For Sgt. First Class Stead, Jan L. Parkinson was now RA 16 962 677 and a file that he could close.

For me, I knew that in ninety days—Wednesday, January 24, 1968—I would be returning to this place to be sworn in before heading to Fort Dix, New Jersey. My head was spinning as I tried to grasp all that I needed to accomplish before then. Much to my surprise, things fell into place more easily than I expected.

Two things were at the top of my agenda: figuring out where Ami would live and finding a place for our stuff that would probably not be used for two years and eight months.

Ami's mother said Ami could live with her, but Ami immediately said, "No way." (I have often thought that one of the reasons she married me was to get away from her mother.)

My folks offered to let Ami live with them. They said she could have the entire upstairs, which included my old bedroom. We all said it would sort of be like having her own apartment, except, of course, it would not be like that at all. All things considered, however, it seemed like the ideal solution.

We stumbled into a much better solution for our apartment and furniture. Ami's younger sister was pregnant, and she and her future husband were looking for a place to live. It was a turnkey operation for them, and we could just walk away without having to move all the furniture or find a place to store it.

The reaction of people at my office was widely varied. To my boss's boss, a former Marine, who had always suspected I was a hippie or a communist (or maybe both) because of my long hair, I was now a person worthy of his respect. However, Betty Stevens, an artist in my department, admitted she was concerned about my safety. She made a "magic circle" talisman that she said would protect me from harm. Harvey Gariety, our art director, made me a simple card that seemed to sum up everyone's expectations (including mine) that the Army and I would not be a great fit. The message on the card was a short quote from Erasmus in 1509: "In the land of the blind, the one-eyed man is king."

Rick Willhardt who had been assigned to the Army Home Town News Office before joining Hallmark as an advertising copy-writer offered the best advice of anyone. He said, "Don't expect anything about the Army to make sense."

The quote proved to be prophetic—at least in my opinion.

People were curious and asked lots of questions—where was I going for basic training, what would my wife be doing, how would we get by on Army pay, when would I get a leave to come home, but the one word that was never mentioned around me was *Vietnam*.

The ninety days slipped by quickly. There was a party at work. Some friends planned a fancy dinner. We moved out of our apartment and into my old bedroom. On my last night at home, we had a quiet dinner with my parents, and later, my dad cut my hair short because I didn't want to have an Army barber do it.

It was a largely sleepless night. In the morning, my dad drove the four of us to the Armed Forces Examining and Entrance Station, where we said our goodbyes.

I walked through the doors and into the Army.

SIX

Welcome to Fort Dix

I t was late when our plane landed in Philadelphia. Six of us from Kansas City were headed to Fort Dix, New Jersey. Because of my perfect score on the qualifying exam—or perhaps because I said I would rather lead a group of men in marching instead of reading a book—I had been put in charge of the group. "Being in charge" simply meant I had to carry six brown envelopes containing our virtually empty personnel files and to make sure all six of us got on the bus to Fort Dix, which was already half full by the time we found it.

Once I was on the bus, I wasn't in charge of anything.

We were tired and anxious to get to the post and get some sleep.

The Army, however, had other ideas.

As we got off the bus, we were greeted by a bunch of drill instructors (DIs) in Smokey the Bear hats who were screaming orders and insults at us. They seemed to be trying to get us into some sort of formation with the sixty other dazed-looking guys already there.

It was chaotic. We wandered around like a bunch of lost cattle, bumping into each other as we were told by one sergeant to do one thing, only to be immediately ordered to do something entirely different by a second, and called "a bunch of worthless fucking assholes" by a third.

Since we had not had time to screw up anything yet, I wondered why we were being harangued by a bunch of total strangers. It appeared to be spontaneous, arbitrary, and totally random harassment. However, it actually was *planned* arbitrary and totally random harassment. It is still the standard greeting for everyone beginning Basic Training in today's volunteer Army. The DIs even have a name for it. Staff Sergeant Kristopher Jackson, a DI writing for a veterans' blog in 2016, offered this explanation:

"What happens when they first arrive, we have this thing called 'The Shark Attack.' We toss in a little bit of confusion at first to kind of put the fear factor in them. We want to go ahead and set confusion and those loud noises out of the gate at the beginning. Once they put that first foot down on the ground, they kind of know what's in store for them."

When our group achieved some semblance of a formation, four drill sergeants holding clipboards moved to the front of the group. One of them pointed to the door of the closest building and announced in a booming voice, "If I call your name, gather all your possessions and move briskly through that door and wait."

When he had split off about a fourth of the herd, a second sergeant took an equal-sized group to another building, and a third sergeant took half of what remained. I ended up in the fourth group and never saw the other five men from Kansas City again. My group was moved to an auditorium where we waited. Eventually, someone shouted, "Attention!"

Most of us had no idea what that meant, so when we responded rather haphazardly, the shouting began again.

A tall sergeant first class who could easily have been a clone of Sgt. First Class Stead in Kansas City marched to the front of the room. From his bearing and stern look, it was obvious he was in charge. He stood silently, staring straight ahead and waited for the remaining DIs to restore order.

I was in the front row. Right in the line of fire, so to speak. As a result, I became a target for a gung-ho Airborne Ranger DI who stopped directly in front of me, the brim of his Smokey the Bear hat no more than a couple of millimeters from my forehead.

"Are you ignoring a direct order, private?" he demanded.

"No, sir," I said.

"What did you say, private?" he shouted in my face.

"No, sir," I said.

"You don't ever call a sergeant 'sir.' Only officers are addressed as 'sir.' You address a sergeant as 'sergeant.' You got that, private?"

"Yes, sergeant."

Then it happened.

The guy standing next to me smiled.

I was off the hook. The sergeant moved on.

"Did I say something funny, private?" he shouted at his new target.

"No, sir," was the response.

The sergeant exploded.

The other shouting in the room abruptly stopped, replaced by an ominous silence. The sharks smelled blood in the water.

"Weren't you paying attention? Or are you deliberately trying to annoy me?"

"No, sergeant."

"No, sergeant, what? 'No,' you weren't listening or 'no,' you were deliberately trying to annoy me?"

In that instant, I learned three valuable lessons about surviving Basic Training:

1. When you are being yelled at, there is no correct answer. You are always wrong.

2. Do whatever you can to blend into the crowd. Avoid standing in the front row if at all possible. The ultimate goal is to become invisible.

3. Don't smile. Ever.

Eventually, we were sufficiently organized (or perhaps they had simply completed the requisite amount of shouting), and it got quiet. The sergeant first class introduced himself as our senior DI and told us that we were now part of Delta Company. With a note of pride in his voice, he announced that we had our own Delta Company yell, and as if it was the most important lesson we could possibly learn in our first day in the Army, we were going to memorize our yell before we did anything else:

Delta! D-E-L-T-A!

Second to none.

We'll get it done.

With sweat and blood.

KILL!

Of course, we weren't loud enough the first time.

"I can't hear you!" our senior DI shouted.

We shouted back half a dozen more times until we were all screaming.

What happened after that was a blur. For the next twenty-four hours or so, Delta Company was on the move. We moved from standing in one line to standing in another line. We never knew where we were going or what we were standing in line for. One line produced a couple of sets of fatigues and another our first round of immunizations. What followed in no particular order was our first Army buzz cut, two pairs of black leather combat boots, a dental exam, our dog tags, a much-used overcoat (which we stood in line again to return a few days later), a second round of shots, and on and on, until finally, we were given a temporary bunk in a transit barracks that was used for guys about to be discharged as well as new troops.

Propped up against my bunk was a duffel bag full of gear that had belonged to someone who obviously wanted to leave everything about his Army experience behind.

The belongings of that unknown soldier immediately made me think of the dead man in Yossarian's tent. It was the first time I wondered if *Catch-22* was a factual account rather than fiction. But it was not the last.

In the middle of the night, we were awakened by more shouting and banging on the walls. We were about to have our first experience on KP (Kitchen Police) where we would spend an unpleasant day working in a noisy mess hall kitchen.

I was one of three men assigned to pots and pans. "P&P" is the second worst job in the mess hall. The worst is cleaning the grease trap. For the next several hours, we stood over a couple of ancient metal sinks filled with hot soapy water and scrubbed mammoth cast-iron frying pans, baking sheets, soup pots, and all manner of utensils. For the first hour or so, we got stuff pretty clean, but when the rush was on, we couldn't keep up with the demand, so we adjusted our standards. Since we didn't have time to change the water, we simply removed the visible scraps of food before returning the pans to the cooks. Occasionally, one of them would shove a particularly nasty looking pot under our noses and bark, "Do you call this clean?" They usually were too busy to care and we didn't either.

When our P&P sentence was over, we returned to the temporary barracks, packed up whatever gear we had at that point, and marched to the brick building that would be our home for the next eight weeks.

While we were getting our new olive-drab wardrobe, a couple rounds of shots, and our first Army haircut, the Vietcong and North Vietnamese Army troops launched the Tet Offensive, a coordinated attack on more than 100 cities, villages, and outposts in South Vietnam, including Saigon. American and South Vietnamese troops were totally surprised.

The North expected the South Vietnamese Army would collapse, the Saigon Government would be overthrown, and the U.S. would end its involvement in the conflict.

None of that happened. The North suffered staggering losses. On the surface, the Tet Offensive was a major military victory for the South, but the extensive news coverage of the massive surprise offensive shocked the American public and eroded public support for the war. So, despite their heavy losses, North Vietnam achieved a strategic victory, and the Tet Offensive marked a turning point in the war.

A few days after the start of Tet, North Korean naval vessels attacked the *USS Pueblo*, an American Navy spy ship operating in neutral waters off the North Korean coast. One American crew member was killed, and the remaining eighty-three were taken prisoner as the *USS Pueblo* was seized and towed to a North Korean port.

Suddenly, the world seemed like a much more dangerous place. However, the members of Delta Company at Fort Dix, New Jersey, did not know any of this. The Army had cut us off completely from the outside world. We were not allowed access to telephones, television, radio, or newspapers. No outside visitors were allowed.

I didn't realize it at the time, but my training had already started. In fact, it started at the moment I stepped off the bus.

SEVEN

The Basics of Basic Training

The Army's official name for the first eight weeks of training is Basic Combat Training, but I never heard anyone use that term. Everyone called it Basic Training or just Basic. That's appropriate because the eight weeks of Basic have a much larger objective than just learning how to shoot people.

Basic Training is where the transformation from civilian life to the military world begins. Although the military today must deal with a vastly different variety of weapons and strategies—from conventional warfare to terrorists and guerilla fighters—the way troops are trained has not changed significantly in the past century or longer.

In other words, Basic is still basic.

In the U.S., our civilian government has the ultimate authority over the military—at least on paper. However, as the size, complexity, and importance of the military increased, so has its control over its own activities. The military's power to influence the discourse and ultimately the decisions of the civilian government has increased its ability to act totally independently.

The military is not a democracy. It has a completely different legal system. Much of the military's activity is hidden behind the curtain of national security. And behind the hundreds of very specific regulations is the "informal system." Or to put it another way, "the way things really work."

There are two primary objectives of Basic Training, but they are never discussed—or even mentioned—to the trainee.

The first objective is to persuade the trainee to forget about the way things worked in their civilian life and be guided by the procedures, principles, and values that best serve the needs of the Army. That objective can be summed up in five words: You're in the Army now.

That idea sounds obvious, and it is. But the difference is far more significant than it appears at first glance. It isn't just taking off your civvies and putting on olive-drab.

Army Basic Training—and the eight weeks of Advanced Individual Training (AIT) that immediately follow—go well beyond simply learning the Army system. You must also unlearn being a civilian. The point of Basic Training is to break down a recruit's sense of identity and create a new identity based entirely on his association with the Army. Psychological conditioning techniques are used to shape attitudes and behaviors so that new soldiers will obey all orders, face mortal dangers, and kill their opponents in battle. When it is described in those terms, you realize that is a monumental change. Another word for it is *brainwashing*.

In short, forget about the way things worked in the civilian world because the Army has a whole different rulebook. At the top of the list and far and away, the most important rule is: "Obey all orders quickly, willingly, and without question."

"Why?" is not part of the military vocabulary. Soldiers do not need to understand the reason behind a particular order. They are just supposed to *do it*. In other words, follow the orders of your superiors and don't ask questions.

There is no lesson plan for instilling this mindset. No classes. No handbooks. But it is part of everything that happens in Basic Training. It is the foundation upon which everything else depends.

The Army's method of establishing this attitude is completely different than the methods in the civilian world. Reason and persuasion are not part of the military equation. The Army teaches by intimidation. The motivation is fear.

Virtually everything in my first eight weeks in the Army was focused on separating me from my civilian life and establishing a new Army persona. The process is not subtle, but at the same time, the intent is not immediately obvious. It is so constant and pervasive that, at times, it starts to feel normal, which, of course, is the Army's goal.

The process starts with a new first name—and it was the same for everyone. We were all addressed as *private*. No one ever used my given first name.

That was convenient for the DIs because they did not have to learn anyone's name or anything at all personal about the men they were training. It is much harder to send someone into a situation where they may be injured or killed if you have a strong personal relationship with them.

EIGHT
Learning to Kill

The first objective of Basic Training—to convert civilian draftees and enlisted men into a cohesive group who would obey all orders quickly, willingly, and without question—is the foundation for the second objective: Learning to kill.

There are actually two distinct aspects of this training:

1. Developing the skills necessary to use weapons or other means to end another person's life.

2. Developing the belief and attitude that in certain situations, killing another person is appropriate, justified, and necessary.

There was nothing subtle about teaching us the various methods of killing someone. It was almost all hands-on learning. We learned how to take apart, reassemble, clean, load, and fire an M14 rifle, despite the fact that American troops in Vietnam no longer used the M14 in combat.

We had hand-to-hand combat and bayonet training, two skills that would probably be of little use in the jungles of Vietnam.

We spent a couple of sessions practicing "quick kill," a technique using a BB gun. A metal disc the size of a quarter was tossed in the air and you had to shoot and hit it without using the sights on the gun. This method was excitedly touted as a new approach to training, but actually, it was a variation of a technique previously known as "instinctive shooting."

Several classroom sessions were devoted to the corollary of weapons training—survival training which in large part was nothing more than basic first aid. The focus, however, was on preserving a soldier's ability to continue fighting rather than preserving his life. In fact, the U.S. Army Medical Department's motto is *To preserve the fighting force.*

We were shown more ways to kill someone than I ever could have imagined when I was growing up trying to emulate Hopalong Cassidy. While our training on how to kill was relatively straight-forward, the attitude of the trainers was far more unsettling. The Army employed a number of strategies to get us to adopt this new attitude about killing. Some were obvious and direct, but more subtle techniques were also used.

The focus on killing began with my very first taste of Army life on the night I arrived at Fort Dix and learned the Delta Company yell:

Delta! D-E-L-T-A!

Second to none.

We'll get it done.

With sweat and blood.

KILL!

It was reinforced several times every day as we marched or ran to meals, between classes or out to one of the firing ranges, keeping time with one of many not-so-subtle cadences:

Band of brothers,

That's what we said,

Mess with us,

We'll shoot you dead.

Band of brothers,

Trained to kill,

If we don't getcha,

Our sisters will.

I'm not sure if the goal was to make *kill* a battle cry or exactly the opposite: use the word so often that it would lose its emotional impact. Whatever the reasoning, the emphasis on killing was pervasive.

A sign on the bulletin board just inside the entrance to our barracks proclaimed:

"WAR IS OUR BUSINESS AND BUSINESS IS GOOD."

Our training session on how to use a bayonet was an example of how a skilled instructor was able to accomplish both aspects of learning how to kill. It began with the basic technique—how to hold the rifle and how and where to thrust the blade to disable the enemy soldier.

"That will stop him, but then you can give it a twist. That will fuck a gook up real good. Now, show me. I want to see it in your eyes that you want to kill these slopes. Imagine these assholes are the fucking VC, and they have just killed your buddy. You wanna fuckin' kill 'em. So, show me your killer's face. Do you have a war yell? Let me hear your war yell."

Officially, the Army does not condone the use of derogatory language or ethnic and racial slurs, but it was an accepted practice in training and on the battlefield. Such slurs suggested that the target was somehow inferior or even subhuman and deserving of scorn. Derogatory or demeaning stereotypes or labels make it easier to hate...and, if possible, kill members of a targeted group.

At another weapons training session, the instructor drove that home in yet another way. "The reason we are all here," he said, "is to learn to be killers. It doesn't matter if you're a grunt, a cook, a truck driver, or even a medic, you will all become killers because the purpose of the Army is to kill or inflict casualties on the enemy."

Many of the instructors enthusiastically embraced this attitude. Others just went along with it, apparently believing that was the way things were, and there was nothing they could do about it.

For me, however, this casual attitude about taking another person's life was deeply disturbing.

On one unseasonably warm morning, we marched out to one of the firing ranges where we would spend the day in one of the dozen or so permanent foxholes honing our skills with the M14 rifle. When one group finished firing a full clip of bullets at the human silhouette targets down range, the trainees would climb out of the hole and the next group would move in.

The man ahead of me had just moved into the foxhole and when the command "Fire when ready" was given, the group started firing. At first, no one noticed a recruit at the far end of the row had slumped down into the hole. Suddenly, the next man in line started shouting, and when one of the instructors saw what was happening, he began hollering, "Cease firing! Cease firing!"

The other DIs rushed to the foxhole where the young trainee had placed the barrel of his rifle under his chin, set the rifle on "automatic," and pulled the trigger.

He had blown his brains out.

The rest of us were moved to some bleachers behind the foxholes while the body was removed and the site was cleaned up.

The senior DI did not know the dead man's name or what had driven him to suicide when he addressed us.

"This private was obviously disturbed about something," he said. "We will notify his family immediately, but right now, the best thing for the rest of you to do is get right back out there and continue with this training exercise."

I never did find out about the man's motive, but I wondered if he was so deeply troubled about the idea of taking someone else's life that it was easier for him to end his own.

We slowly filed out of the bleachers and formed new lines waiting for our turn to fire at the targets.

We were indeed learning how to kill. And we were learning about the value the Army placed on human life.

NINE

Sick Call

Delta Company was housed in a nondescript brick building that in another location could easily have been mistaken for a factory, public housing, or a minimum-security correctional center. Inside, however, the décor was definitely mid-century American reform school.

There were eight men in each small room, so there were eight identical metal-frame beds and eight gunmetal gray lockers. Nothing on the walls. No chairs. No desks. No tables.

We were required to keep the windows open at least twelve inches at the bottom and another twelve inches at the top. If we dared to close the windows because the rain or snow was blowing into the room, the sergeant who had night duty would wake up all eight of us to reopen the four windows.

The purpose was to keep fresh air circulating so we wouldn't get sick.

It was February in New Jersey.

We all got sick.

During Basic Training, sick call was like a three-hour vacation. It's not that there was anything enjoyable or even remotely pleasant about going on sick call. But compared to what the rest of the company was likely doing for the three hours while you were sitting in a crowded clinic waiting room with twenty or thirty contagious soldiers, sick call seemed to be a pretty good deal.

On a typical February morning at Fort Dix, Delta Company would often start the day running a couple of miles in the rain or snow to a firing range where we would lie down in the mud and fire a couple of clips of ammo at some poorly drawn targets that looked vaguely oriental. On those days, sick call became a very popular option.

The sick call roster was compiled every day after the morning formation. After breakfast, the dozen or so from Delta Company on the list headed for a clinic that served three or four other companies of men currently in Basic Training. The clinic was primarily staffed by medical corpsmen. We were told that there were nurses and doctors on staff, but I never saw one in the half dozen times I went on sick call.

Treatment was very standardized. A corpsman had two pieces of medical equipment: a jar full of thermometers and a clipboard. When a patient showed up, a corpsman checked to make sure the man's name was on the list. Then he gave each patient a thermometer and told them to find a seat and keep the thermometer in their mouth.

The wait might take twenty minutes or more, but eventually, a corpsman would call a name from his list and the patient would walk up to the desk with the thermometer still in his mouth. The corpsman would read and record the temperature before sending the ailing trainee back to an examining room.

Almost every patient had a cold, bronchitis, pneumonia, or something from that family of ailments. The corpsman conducting the examination asked why the trainee was there and regardless of how detailed the patient's explanation was, the corpsman simply wrote "URI" (Upper Respiratory Infection) on the chart and gave each patient an identical package of medicine: aspirin, sore throat lozenges, and nonprescription cough medicine. As nearly as I could determine, the patient's temperature determined whether or not their diagnosis and treatment would be upgraded, but no one knew for sure what the magic numbers were.

According to rumors passed along by frequent sick call visitors, if your temperature was less than 99.8, you were marked "return to duty." If it was 100° or more, you were given twenty-four hours of bedrest. If your temperature was 102° or more, you were sent to the post hospital.

Everyone hoped they would get a number in the sweet spot—just barely over 100°—high enough to extend your "vacation" to twenty-four hours of bed rest, but low enough to avoid a stay in the hospital.

There were a number of ways that trainees tried to beat the system. One morning at sick call, I noticed the guy sitting next to me had removed the thermometer from his mouth and was holding it in the flame of a cigarette lighter.

When the corpsman finally called his name, he took one look at the man's thermometer and gasped.

"106," he said.

The patient had obviously overplayed his hand.

The corpsman handed the patient a new thermometer and ordered him to sit where he could easily be observed.

"You've got five minutes to get that thermometer up to 106° or you are going to see the captain about an Article 15 (an offense that allows a commanding officer to decide innocence or guilt and administer punishment without a hearing)."

However, that was not the strangest occurrence I saw on sick call. That prize goes to two guys who claimed they had tried to commit suicide.

The first had initially come to the clinic to be treated for URI. But he was more troubled than was immediately apparent. He was given the standard medical package for a cold and was told he should take two aspirin every four hours. He reported that he had tried to commit suicide by taking four at one time and was confused why he did not die.

The second man had made a more spectacular effort, but without any more success.

One night, he decided to hang himself. He climbed on to the heating unit by one of the windows in his barracks room. He tied the cords of the Venetian blinds around his neck and jumped. He landed on the floor, and the blinds came crashing down on top of him. The other men in his room who had been sleeping soundly were startled awake by all the noise.

I don't know what became of these three, but if the Army had any sense, they would have sent all three of them home.

The second most common medical problem that brought trainees to the clinic was pain resulting from an injury—most often a sprain or pulled muscle. Surprisingly, the standard treatment for mild-to-moderate pain at the clinic was Darvon. It was a narcotic and an opioid, but it was liberally dispensed by the corpsmen without a prescription and without having seen a doctor. I would estimate that at least a third of the members of Delta Company eventually had their own little bottle of Darvon pills.

I never saw a doctor or a nurse when I was on sick call, but once or twice a week for the first month of Basic Training, a full entourage of medical professionals visited Delta Company to conduct some sort of research study. We were each given a small medicine cup containing what appeared to be a saline solution. We gargled the liquid and then spit it into a tube.

Each time this group showed up, I asked one of the doctors what they were testing for, and the answer was always the same: "I don't know."

My most frequent contact with the medical corps for the first few weeks was with immunization teams. I have no idea how many things I was vaccinated for because at that time, the Army was using jet injection guns. The vaccine was forced through the skin by a burst of compressed air at 1,200 psi. It was a quick and efficient system because more than one vaccine could be administered at a time.

Despite the convenience and efficiency of the jet gun injections, there were safety concerns as well. If the person receiving the injection flinches as the jet gun is being activated or if the corpsman doesn't get the nozzle of the gun butted up straight against the arm, the stream of liquid at such high pressure could tear a serious gash in the skin. Studies also indicate that because injectors can easily become contaminated, the hepatitis C rate among soldiers in Vietnam was five times the general population.

As a result, the military stopped using the jet injection in 1997.

TEN

No Privacy for Privates

There were no secrets in the Army. We had absolutely no privacy or control over our environment. The door to our room in the barracks had to remain open. A DI or any other member of the staff could enter unannounced at any time for any reason or no reason at all.

There were no doors on the stalls in the latrines. We took communal showers.

We marched—or ran—together to and from all of our meals.

I was never alone.

I also had a number: RA 16 962 677. RA stood for "Regular Army." Delta Company was mostly RAs, but we also had a number of NGs (National Guard) and a few ERs (Enlisted Reserves). As I recall, all of the NGs were from the South and they were all White.

Our numbers were supposedly used for identification, but we were often asked to recite our number for no apparent reason. For example, when we marched to the mess hall for meals, there was always a junior officer—usually a fresh new second lieutenant—seated at a table by the door. You gave him your service number, and he did absolutely nothing with the information.

As much as possible, all recruits looked the same. We had the same haircut—a buzz cut—and we were all clean shaven. We all dressed alike because we had all been issued the same uniforms: olive-drab fatigues and ball caps, fatigue jackets, and even identical underwear—white cotton boxer shorts. Those of us who wore glasses were issued two pairs of identical nondescript prescription eyeglasses. We were also given two pairs of black leather combat boots and told that we could not wear the same pair two days in a row. Because they were identical, we had to paint a white dot about the size of a dime on the back of one pair. That made it possible for us to tell them apart, but it also made it easy for the DIs to tell who was not following their orders.

For the first few weeks at the morning formation, a DI would walk behind the rows of trainees looking for anyone who was wearing the wrong boots. If you were wearing "white dots" on "no dot" day—or vice versa—your morning began with a DI screaming obscenities and ordering you to "drop and give me twenty-five (pushups)."

The idea of having everyone look the same was frequently carried to extremes. Every day an order was issued establishing "The Uniform of the Day." It stated exactly what everyone would wear all day. If the weather changed during the day, you could not change what you were wearing until a new Uniform of the Day order was issued.

One day when we were on an outdoor firing range, it started to snow. In the early afternoon, it changed to rain. After we were thoroughly soaked and our boots covered with mud, a new Uniform of the Day was issued. We all had to put on our rubber galoshes and rain ponchos at which point it stopped raining.

The Uniform of the Day did not allow you to have anything in your pockets. The one exception was cigarettes. When we had a break, one of the DIs would call out "Take five. Smoke 'em if you've got 'em." And if you didn't have 'em, there was nothing for you to do except stand around *with your hands out of your pockets.* (DIs went ballistic if they saw you standing around with your hands in your pockets!)

I tried to fill the time by writing letters, keeping a journal in a small spiral notebook, or reading a paperback book. However, as soon as a DI spotted me doing any of those things, the items were confiscated. And to make matters worse, this made me very visible. (Remember Survival Lesson 2? *Do whatever you can to blend into the crowd. Avoid standing in the front row if at all possible. The ultimate goal is to become invisible.*)

I made one last attempt to use those tiny chunks of personal time: I had been given a pocket-sized New Testament by Chaplain Edward Sterling, the minister who led the one Episcopalian service on the post each week. I tried reading that. It did not take long for one of the DIs to notice I was reading during a smoking break. But when he discovered what I was reading, he got very nervous.There was a hastily called conference between the sergeants. It immediately became clear that no one wanted to be the guy who confiscated a soldier's Bible.

Ultimately, they decided I could keep the Bible, but it had to stay in my pocket during smoking breaks. It was a typical Army solution, It did not satisfy anyone. Rick Willhardt's advice put it in perspective: "Don't expect anything about the Army to make sense."

Everything we owned, were issued, or used was identical to everyone else's stuff. Our bunks, sheets, pillows, and itchy olive-drab wool blankets were the same. All of our gear was placed in our lockers according to a prescribed layout. Fatigues hung on the left, dress greens on the right with the left sleeve facing out. For me the most telling symbol of sameness was the space in the locker layout that was labeled "Personal Items." It was four inches by four inches on the bottom shelf.

We were not allowed to have "contraband" in our lockers—even in our personal space. Contraband usually meant food. Food from home—most often cookies—was especially egregious.

Unannounced locker inspections took place during the day when we were out of the barracks. If something turned up in the inspection, you found out about it when you returned to the barracks at the end of the day and everything in your locker had been dumped on the floor.

During one especially vigorous locker inspection, all the lockers were pulled away from the wall. A live grenade wrapped in newspaper was found behind one of the eight lockers in my room. I was glad it was not my locker, but all eight of us were immediately pulled out of the day's training activities and hauled in front of the senior DI who interrogated us one at a time.

When it was my turn to be questioned, the grenade and the newspapers it had been wrapped in were on the desk in front of the sergeant. I told him that I did not have any knowledge of how the grenade got there, and that I was certain none of the other seven assigned to the room would have brought it to the barracks.

I noticed that the newspapers looked old, so I asked the DI what the date on the papers was. He looked at the papers and saw that they were all more than a year old.

I pointed out that none of us would have had twelve-month-old newspapers at our disposal, so we could not have put the grenade there. In other words, the grenade had probably been behind the locker for months. He looked somewhat skeptical but at the same time relieved because this had not happened on his watch.

He called our group together and told us he could not prove or disprove that we had anything to do with the grenade. "For now, I'll assume you are innocent," he said. "But I'm going to keep my eye on each one of you. You're dismissed."

His tone was serious throughout the interrogation, so we had our somber faces on when we left the room, but outside we were almost giddy with relief.

We knew we were innocent, but we had learned that military justice started with a presumption of guilt. Getting past that initial conclusion is often virtually impossible, because the DI is the prosecutor, judge, and jury. The verdict is issued, sentence pronounced, and the punishment administered on the spot. The often-quoted line "Military justice is to justice what military music is to music" certainly rings true.

If you were late to roll call, wore the same boots two days in a row, had a spot on your uniform, or didn't get your required weekly buzz cut, you were guilty of insubordination. The punishment was usually not extreme, but it was almost always accompanied by a dose of humiliation. If the sentence was twenty-five pushups, they took place in front of the entire company who counted them out loud. Occasionally, the guilty man then had to low crawl back to his spot in the formation.

There were always threats of what the Army felt was more serious punishment. When you went on sick call, for example, the DI in charge for the day would remind you that if you missed too much training, you would be held back. In other words, you would have to start Basic Training all over again. That didn't seem to really worry anyone, but the warning was repeated frequently.

The most serious threat was delivered indirectly.

Every morning, we ran to breakfast in formation, keeping in step with one of several call-and-respond cadence chants, such as:

DI: "I want to go to Vietnam."

Troop response: "I want to go to Vietnam."

DI: "I want to kill some Vietcong."

Troop response: "I want to kill some Vietcong."

(Repeat a couple of dozen times)

Our route varied, but we always managed to pass by the stockade. The building looked like dozens of others on the post, except this one which was surrounded by a fifteen-foot chain link fence topped with razor wire.

Over the gate was a large sign that proclaimed: OBEDIENCE TO THE LAW IS FREEDOM.

It didn't make sense to me at the time, and it doesn't make sense to me now. Yet somehow, the threat was clear: "Follow orders or we will lock you up."

However, as the war in Vietnam intensified, a growing number of U.S. soldiers openly protested against the war. One of the largest protests involved more than 100 soldiers imprisoned in the Fort Dix stockade.

The internal protest movement appeared to reveal a significant weakness in the Army's inflexible training regimen. It relied primarily on intimidation to produce soldiers who appeared to be unquestioningly loyal to the chain of command system. Obviously, it didn't work on everyone...including me.

What was clearly missing in my weeks of training at Fort Dix was any discussion of the Army's overall mission or our objective in Vietnam.

In the civilian world, inspiring commitment and loyalty to a cause, an organization, a company, or an ideology would start with a positive mission statement or objective that an individual would willingly embrace.

Our leaders in Washington talked about a strategy of winning the hearts and minds of the Vietnamese people. They said we were fighting to stop the spread of Communism in Southeast Asia and to preserve freedom and democracy for the citizens of South Vietnam.

They told the American people we were winning. America always wins because we are the good guys.

True or not, these messages were never part of the training for the new soldiers of Delta Company. Someone must have decided that there was no need to waste time trying to convince us that there was a sound reason for us to be fighting in Vietnam or that ultimately something positive would result from our effort.

Perhaps, the military leaders realized nobody would believe the pronouncements from Washington. The closest anyone at Fort Dix ever came to an explanation was the frequently repeated phrase that "Vietnam is not a great war, but it's the only war we have."

Actually, it's pretty simple if you let it be. You obey orders. You follow the rules. You don't ask questions. You become a soldier.

They tell you your job is to kill people. And they will let you know which ones.

Now that I was part of the military, I had to play by their rules. As my training continued, this became more and more disturbing.

ELEVEN

God and/or Country

I was one of those kids who played by the rules. I did what was expected of me by my parents, teachers, and other adults—the authority figures of my growing-up years.

I grew up in the Presbyterian Church. Or more to the point, the Presbyterian church down the street from our house. I took part in Sunday school, Vacation Bible School, and the children's and youth choirs. But it was the dynamic young minister and his positive message that had attracted my parents to this energetic new church. And since my parents were Presbyterians, I was a Presbyterian too.

Like many of my contemporaries, my faith journey had not been a straight line leading directly to a rock-solid set of beliefs. It has been a haphazard wandering, picking up pieces here and there, keeping what seemed to fit at the moment, and discarding what did not. My beliefs had not been static. They were constantly examined and questioned, and they continue to evolve.

In college, I sampled a few other churches—from Southern Baptist (I had a friend who was financing his education by serving as the organist there) to the other end of the spectrum, Unitarian, which another friend described as "religion lite." I briefly joined the Campus Crusade for Christ (too conservative). I got a wider and more academic view when I took a college course called simply "Religion." It was essentially a comparative religion course. But it was taught by a Jesuit priest, so most of the comparing was every major faith in the world vs. Catholicism. In his classroom, Catholicism always won.

When Ami and I began dating, I started attending her small Episcopalian church in Kansas City. The mix of ritual and doctrine fit who I was and what I needed at that stage of my life. I signed up for their prospective member class that met every Sunday night for about three months.

The Episcopalians were a fairly diverse group which appealed to me. If they had room for the outspoken California Bishop James Pike, who championed the ordination of women, racial desegregation, a living wage for all workers, and acceptance of gay and lesbian members in mainline churches, they surely had room for me. I became an Episcopalian at Grace and Holy Trinity Cathedral in Kansas City. It was a moving ceremony that concluded with the laying on of hands by the bishop with every new member.

The one constant in my religious journey has been accepting Jesus as a role model. To me, that is what it means to call yourself a Christian: to follow his teachings and to attempt to pattern your life after the values and examples in his.

When my son died and the draft board changed my classification to I-A, I knew it would mean disrupting my life, leaving my wife and job, and discarding the vision of my future that I had brought with me when I graduated from college. I explored every option available to avoid this change, but when I realized there were none short of going to Canada, I felt compelled to fulfill a responsibility to my country.

I never imagined that loyalty to my country would conflict with my Christian faith. After all, I had been taught from an early age that we are "the good guys." We entered wars reluctantly and always with the best possible motives.

The Army itself convinced me I was wrong.

I never expected to like being in the Army, but I thought if I could just do my time, it would satisfy any obligation to my country and eventually allow me to reclaim my place in the real world.

But the Army wanted more than my reluctant participation. It expected me to leave my civilian ideas and values behind and adopt "the Army way," which meant learning how to manage violence and to kill other human beings who had been labeled as enemies.

As my training progressed, I steadily grew more uneasy about what my responsibility as a soldier would be. The seed had been planted by that single statement in the OCS brochure: *An officer's primary responsibility is the management of violence.*

My exposure to Army life, methods, and values allowed that seed to sprout and take root. There was no "aha" moment, no single incident when I suddenly decided I was a conscientious objector. Instead, I realized that the Army had gradually been revealing its true self.

Once my eyes were opened, I could see other examples that pointed in the same direction.

The way the Pentagon glorified body counts was one of the most obvious. The number of killed or wounded had become the American scorecard for the war in Vietnam. If in a single skirmish, a single day, or an entire month more North Vietnamese and Vietcong soldiers were killed or wounded than the number of American troops killed or wounded, it was counted as a victory. South Vietnamese troops were an insignificant part of the score keeping. The numbers on the military's charts and graphs were no longer human beings. They were points toward declaring a winner in a brutal game.

By the time I finished Basic Training and was assigned to another company for Advanced Individual Training (AIT), it was clear to me that my faith outweighed any obligation I had to my country.

At their General Convention in 1934, the Episcopal Church adopted this statement to clarify their position on conscientious objection: "It is the duty of Christians to put the Cross above the flag, and in any conflict of loyalties, unhesitatingly to follow the Christ."

What I could or would do about that conflict, however, was not at all clear.

TWELVE
Advanced Individual
Training (AIT)

Every new soldier regardless of their future military specialty gets the same dose of Basic Training. The emphasis is on preparing everyone for combat. After completing eight weeks of Basic, everyone is assigned to Advanced Individual Training (AIT) for additional training in a designated specialty.

My so-called specialty was infantry, the largest and least specialized specialty the Army has to offer. Nearly every post that provides Basic Training also provides AIT for infantry. So, I remained at Fort Dix and was assigned to Alpha Company, Third Battalion, First AIT Brigade.

Everyone in Alpha Company was headed for the infantry and most likely an assignment in Vietnam. To the casual observer AIT looked like more of the same, but the changes were more significant than they appeared to be at first glance. A lot of new faces filled the slots left vacant by those who had been transferred to one of the Army's special schools.

That meant that my AIT training was focused on the skills needed to become an infantryman (or a grunt, which I had learned early on is the term others use for a foot soldier). Infantry AIT meant more weapons training plus tactics and procedures.

We were introduced to an array of new weapons systems including:

- The M18A1 Claymore mine, a recent innovation that fired several hundred metal pellets at one time to create a kill zone about 165-feet wide and seven-feet high.
- The M79 grenade launcher, a shoulder-fired weapon that could fire a forty-six-mm grenade about 250 meters.
- The M1911A1 .45-caliber sidearm.
- The belt-fed .50-caliber machine gun that could fire 450 to 600 rounds a minute.

We never actually fired any of these weapons. We were just shown how to use them.

I often wondered how confident the average American soldier would be when he arrived in Vietnam (or any war zone) without ever actually using any of the weapons that he would be expected to utilize.

In AIT, we also learned about conducting patrols, setting up an ambush, and moving through the jungles of Vietnam. Of course, we had to use a forested area in New Jersey as a substitute for the jungle.

But even in the make-believe jungles of New Jersey with outdated M14 rifles, the message for me was real. I would soon be expected to pick up an M16 rifle and set out to kill people I did not know.

For AIT, we were housed in a World War II-era wooden barracks building that had been pressed into service to handle the steadily increasing demand for troops in Vietnam. Both floors of the two-story building were open spaces packed with two-man bunk beds. Nearly twice as many troops were crowded into the old barracks than had been housed there when the buildings were new. Trainees were allowed to have a radio, and every morning at 6:00 a.m., WFIL, the Philadelphia AM rock station, played The Rascals' hit "A Beautiful Morning." The song was met with insults and raunchy epithets from those who didn't appreciate the irony.

Our platoon leader, Sgt. Morales, occupied the one private room on the first floor. His presence in the barracks and his personality was major change from the DIs in Basic who shouted every instruction and berated you for every misstep. Showering, shaving, and using the latrine with someone at 6:00 a.m. can be a great equalizer.

Sgt. Morales was a very friendly guy who was always eager to start a conversation...especially if it was about him. Unfortunately, English was a second language for Morales...and a distant second at that. Sometimes, his words were not English or Spanish, and it was difficult to figure out what he was trying to say.

For example, he liked to tell stories about his days with the U.S. Army in Southeast Asia. "I loved Thighland. It was a beautiful country," he said.

Early on the morning of April 5, 1968, I was in the shower when Morales came in.

"Well, I guess they killed Martin Luther," he said matter-of-factly.

"What?" I asked.

"Martin Luther," he said. "They killed him."

I had no idea what he was talking about, but I didn't want to say Luther had been dead for more than 400 years, so I just made a vaguely positive grunt of agreement.

Later when I heard a newscast on the radio, I realized Morales was talking about the assassination of Dr. Martin Luther King Jr. in Memphis the night before. The murder of Dr. King put everyone on edge. There would certainly be demonstrations, and some of them would turn violent. Because Newark, the closest big city, was considered a likely trouble spot, all of our scheduled training for the day was cancelled. We spent the afternoon marching in a tight wedge formation up and down an empty street on the post as if we were breaking up an imaginary riot.

Fortunately, we were not needed. We had not been adequately trained and did not have any weapons, protective clothing, or gasmasks. We would not have been able to break up a crowd of five-year-old kids on Big Wheels.

A couple of weeks later, the musical group *Up With People* had scheduled performances in Newark, and one of their concerts was designated "Military Appreciation Night." Our AIT company was asked to provide some soldiers for the audience. I was one of thirty or so soldiers from Alpha Company who were "volunteered" to attend. We put on our dress uniforms and climbed into the back of one of three two-and-a-half-ton trucks for a ninety-minute ride to the theater in Newark to be appreciated.

Our route to the theater took us through a depressed neighborhood, but it was a warm night and Black families were relaxing on the steps in front of their apartment buildings. One of the mothers noticed us right away, and a look of alarm appeared on her face. She grabbed her young daughter and ran up the stairs shouting a warning to her neighbors: "THE ARMY'S COMING! THE ARMY'S COMING!"

The other parents started gathering their kids and hustling them inside.

Some of the kids were confused.

Some were scared.

Some cried.

It only took a few minutes for our trucks to exit the residential neighborhood, but by the time we had moved into a commercial area, the sidewalks and the stairs in front of the apartments were completely empty.

After that, none of us really felt appreciated.

THIRTEEN

Now What?

Mahatma Gandhi said, "To believe in something and not to live it is dishonest." In other words, the next step was up to me.

I had made a decision. I would not use a weapon against another human being. I would not be a soldier.

However, one does not simply resign from the Army and walk away. Quite the opposite. Most who have attempted that are court-martialed and tossed in into the stockade. That seemed to be the most likely result for me too.

What were my options? Did I even have any meaningful alternatives?

I had another two months of training at Fort Dix before I was assigned somewhere else—quite likely Vietnam—where my decision would be put to the test almost immediately.

Until then, I could just play along with the daily training regimen and hope a miracle would occur that would save me from having to face the consequences of my decision.

I could go AWOL and try to stay hidden for the rest of my life or emigrate to Canada.

I could wait for an opportunity in a future weapons training session and refuse to participate.

Or I could take a more proactive approach and inform someone in the chain of command—most likely the company commander— that I was a conscientious objector and I would no longer handle weapons—even in training exercises. To further complicate my situation, there was no one at Fort Dix for me to talk to about my options.

I did meet a couple of times with Chaplain Edward Sterling. He tried to be helpful and sympathetic, but every time we met, he was in uniform and our conversations always left me with the impression that the silver oak leaves on his shoulder were as important to him as the silver crosses on his collar.

I didn't know anyone in the civilian world with the knowledge or experience to offer meaningful advice. And even if there were someone, contact with them would be limited as long as I was in Basic Training. Mail was frustratingly slow. Trying to make a phone call was difficult and expensive. There were only three pay phones outside the barracks and a couple of hundred guys who wanted to use them.

Almost all my calls were to my wife, Ami, in Kansas City. She became my sounding board, my confidante, my voice, and my Google research. We discussed my next step and concluded that I should request a meeting with the company commander and lay it all out for him and see where that ended up.

In the meantime, she continued to look for other possibilities. She made contact with a Mennonite peace group in Kansas

City, who told her about the Episcopal Peace Fellowship, a ministry of the Episcopal Church in the United States that promoted peace initiatives and helped individuals inside and outside the military to establish their conscientious objector status. The information they provided changed everything for me.

The Army seems to have a regulation for just about everything, so I should not have been surprised to discover there was a regulation establishing a protocol for dealing with conscientious objectors in the Army.

Sure enough, the Army had one that did exactly that: AR 635-20 Personnel Separation—Conscientious Objection.

The regulation allowed an individual who enlisted in the Army and had subsequently become a conscientious objector to apply for a change of status to noncombatant and become a medic or to be released from the Army to perform civilian alternative service, such as hospital orderly.

The applicant's belief had to be faith-based and had to have been developed after joining the Army. Draftees were not eligible. The application required a lengthy personal history, a description of the source of the belief, and three interviews: an Army chaplain, a psychiatrist, and an investigating officer. The applicant could also attach letters of support or explanation. Once an applicant had declared he was a conscientious objector, the regulation required that he be removed from military duties and remain with his current unit until a decision was reached on his completed application.

I contacted Rev. Tom Hayes, the executive director of the Episcopal Peace Fellowship in Philadelphia, and he provided me a copy of the regulation and a list of questions that I would have to answer. He also counseled me on how to deal with the process. He also suggested that I collect as many letters of support as possible. He added a note of caution: of the 1,300 applicants during the previous year, more than 85 percent were denied.

I took his advice and cautions to heart, but for the moment at least, I had an option to pursue even if the odds were against me.

FOURTEEN

The Management of Violence

The regulation dealing with conscientious objection described all of the steps required to complete my application for release from the Army. All except one anyway. It did not offer any clues about how to begin the process.

During Basic, there had been so much emphasis on the chain of command, I figured if I asked anyone about the first step, their answer would be "talk to your immediate superior." That would have been Sgt. Morales. I was certain that Morales would not have any idea what I was talking about, and we would quickly be embroiled in a communications disaster, so I decided to approach the company commander, Captain Douglas. For some reason, he was not available when I went to the office. Rather than asking me to come back later, the company clerk, who had not asked the reason for my request, called the battalion commander and arranged for me to see him immediately. I had never seen this man—a major—and I didn't even know his name, so neither one of us knew what to expect.

I realized that announcing I was a conscientious objector to a senior Army officer was not likely to produce a positive response. I decided to limit the scope of this first meeting to informing him that

SOLDIER WITHOUT A GUN

I had decided I wanted to drop OCS. I thought that would be fairly easy to explain. As an officer, I would have to serve eight months longer than the standard two-year enlistment. So I said I was anxious to return to my wife and our civilian life together.

Initially, the major took the news calmly. He did not seem especially upset that I had decided that I did not want to be an officer, but he wanted to know why I had changed my mind. He repeated many of the arguments that Sgt. First Class Stead had offered a few months earlier in Kansas City.

My answers didn't satisfy the major, and he continued to push for more information. Eventually I said, "I understand that an officer's primary responsibility is the management of violence. I don't want that kind of responsibility."

"What?" he said. This was obviously a new term to him. "That doesn't make any sense. Where did you get that crazy idea?"

"I read it in an Army brochure about Officer Candidate School," I said.

The major just stared at me for what seemed like minutes.

"That's impossible," he said. "You must have read it wrong or remembered it wrong. I don't suppose you just happen to have that brochure with you," he said.

"No, sir," I said.

It was obvious that without the brochure, this discussion was not going to go anywhere. The major had his clerk type up the necessary form to remove my name from the OCS list and I signed it.

I expected someone would want to talk to me about quitting OCS, but days passed without any discussion of my meeting with the major. It became apparent that once I decided I did not want to be an officer, the Army didn't want me to be one either.

However, I was puzzled that throughout my time in the Army, I was apparently the only one who had ever seen the term "management of violence." Surely anyone who had chosen the Army as their career would have noticed it. Every time I came across a new bit of Army literature, I read it, but I never found the term again in any Army-produced material. I began to wonder if I had imagined it.

Years later, the creation of the internet and search engines like Google made it possible for me to solve the mystery.

The concept was first set forth in Harvard professor and noted political scientist Samuel P. Huntington's book *The Soldier and the State: Theory and Policies of Civil-Military Relations* (Belknap Press, 1957). In fact, the term was widely used by senior military leaders to support the argument that military officers are "professionals" comparable to professionals in business and government. Recognition of officers as professionals was considered essential to the establishment of a permanent professional military that was not dependent on the draft.

In his book, Huntington states "the modern officer corps is a professional body and the modern officer a professional man." He defines the three qualities of a professional as:

1. Expertise
2. Responsibility
3. Corporateness

He contends that the officer corps conforms to this definition by "displaying specialized knowledge in the management of violence, maintaining a monopoly on education and advancement in their field, and has an overarching responsibility to the society they serve." The military profession requires comprehensive study, training, and expertise in an intellectual set of skills including organizing of forces and planning, executing and directing activities to become an officer.

He points out that the military expertise necessary for the management of violence includes the science of war and combat as well as organizational and administrative skills. In addition, each step up in the hierarchy of the military profession demands more responsibility and skill because they are authorized to make more strategic decisions.

In contrast, Huntington said that enlisted personnel have neither the intellectual skills nor the professional responsibility of the officer. They are specialists in the application of violence, but not the management of violence. Their vocation is a trade not a profession.

In 1968, there was nothing else I could do to clear up the confusion about "managing violence." I simply would not bring it up again.

My immediate concern was deciding how and when I was going to declare that I was a conscientious objector. I finally decided that the next payday would be a good time to announce my beliefs in a way that I hoped would be an example of my sincerity.

FIFTEEN

The Line

The line stretched from the small wooden table that had been moved to the center of the mess hall, out the door, and outside into the company street. It moved slowly toward the young lieutenant, now nameless and faceless in my memory, who was seated at the table where a metal box filled with envelopes containing cash had been placed.

A .45-caliber pistol was strapped to the lieutenant's hip in the unlikely event someone would try to make off with the meager payroll of a company of new recruits on a large U.S. Army post.

The pistol was simply a part of the ritual, like the words I would be expected to recite when I took my turn in front of the lieutenant:

"Private Parkinson, Jan L., RA 16 962 677. I respectfully request my pay, sir."

Now with only a few minutes until I would be at the head of the line, I was scared.

The feeling was not unlike my first time on the high diving board at the city pool. Once I had stepped onto the ladder, the line of eager, experienced divers in front of and behind me seemed to be carrying me up to the end of the diving board, where I would either jump or turn and make my way off the platform and face the humiliation of failing to live up to my own expectations.

On that day, I jumped and landed safely in ten feet of water.

Now standing in another line, a lot more was at stake. I had a good reason to be scared. I was about to break the Army's most basic rule: the chain of command. A soldier is expected to obey any order from a superior. Questions or differing opinions were not tolerated. Dissent would be squashed.

I was not only going to dissent. I was about to question the morality of the Army's mission and methods as well as its very existence.

When it was my turn in front of the young lieutenant, he did not even look up from the list in front of him on the table.

"Next," he said.

"Private Parkinson, Jan L., RA 16 962 677. I respectfully decline to accept my pay, sir," I said.

The lieutenant was slow to react. He looked up and stared at me for what felt like an eternity.

"What?" he said finally.

"Private Parkinson, Jan L., RA…"

"You can't do that!" he said emphatically.

"Why?" I asked. "With all due respect, sir, if it is my money, it should be my choice whether I accept it or not."

"Well, it's not your money. It's the Army's money until you accept it. It's my job to give it to you, and it's your job to take it," he said. "And what am I supposed to do with it if you don't take it?" he asked.

"I don't know, sir," I said. "It is not my place to say."

"What the god-damned-hell are you up to?" he said. "Why are you doing whatever it is you are trying to do?"

"Since I have been in the Army, my training has been focused on teaching me how to kill people and to better equip me—mentally and physically—to do that," I said. "I have come to believe that taking someone's life is not justifiable for any reason. It would be unchristian and immoral—a betrayal of my religious beliefs—for me to accept money for that."

We were now in uncharted territory. Neither of us knew what was next, but the lieutenant knew he would have to do something. Nothing in his training had prepared him for this.

He stared at me and then at the men still in line who were growing more impatient as they waited to be paid.

He looked back at me and trying his best to sound decisive, he said, "Sit over there," pointing to a row of wooden chairs by the door.

"When I'm finished here, I'll take you to see Captain Douglas."

He had decided to make me someone else's problem. All I could do was wait and see what would happen next.

SIXTEEN

The Road to Damascus

Captain Douglas was our company commander. Facing him was like being sent to the principal's office. In both cases, I didn't know what to expect on the other side of the door. The fear of the unknown was the most intimidating aspect, especially since I always anticipated the worst possible outcome.

Captain Douglas himself, however, was certainly not physically intimidating. He was very short—perhaps just an inch or two above the minimum height of sixty inches. Except for a brief appearance on our first day of training, I can only recall seeing him one other time. That was after the company had spent a couple of days doing nothing but cleaning and polishing anything that didn't move to prepare for a big-deal inspection that had all the officers and drill sergeants on edge. The morning after the inspection, Captain Douglas came out of his office long enough to give us the results.

"We passed the inspection," he announced, as if he were personally responsible. "And the inspection team gave us a special commendation for the cleanliness of our latrines. Now it may sound a little silly to you, but that made me proud to be your commanding officer."

He was right. It sounded silly.

But when I was ushered into his office after refusing to accept my pay, it was anything but silly.

After the obligatory exchange of salutes, his first words made it clear that we were not going to be having a meeting. It was a confrontation. A full-on assault.

"So where were you on the road to Damascus when this revelation suddenly occurred?" he demanded. "Did the clouds part and God speak directly to you? Sounds to me like that's what you're saying. You do know about Saint Paul on the road to Damascus, don't you? Is that what happened to you? Are you like Saint Paul?"

All this without a pause to take a breath.

I attempted to explain that this decision was not a sudden revelation, a vision, or a divine intervention, but a process of discernment that began when I entered the Army nearly four months earlier. In fact, it was the training I received from the Army itself that led me to the conclusion that for me to take another person's life would be an act of moral arrogance. Killing for any reason was inconsistent with my beliefs.

"What is your religion?" Captain Douglas asked.

"Episcopalian."

"That's interesting," he said, "because I'm an Episcopalian."

In other words, one of us must be wrong. Since he was a captain and I was a private, his interpretation must be the correct one.

Great, I thought. I have already told him that his chosen profession is immoral. Now I have questioned his religion too.

This was not going well.

He challenged every statement I made, hoping to trip me up. And he kept coming back to the Damascus question.

He threatened me with a myriad of possible outcomes—all bad. If I persisted, I could expect a dishonorable discharge; diminished career opportunities; negative impact on my family, my friends, and my marriage; loss of veteran's benefits; jail; and my personal favorite: I could not re-enlist.

In retrospect, I'm grateful he took that approach. It made it easier to stand my ground. After half an hour of constant ranting, he became exasperated with my refusal "to listen to reason" and gave up.

"Go up to the barracks and get all your gear," he said. "Come directly back here. Do not talk to anyone. Do not answer any questions. Just get your gear, get your ass back here, and report to the sergeant in the office. Starting tonight, you'll bunk in the room upstairs."

"Tomorrow morning, you don't go to roll call. You report to this office. Your job from now on will be to complete the paperwork you have to submit to Washington if you want to be considered a conscientious objector.

"But I can guarantee you this: you don't have a chance in hell of it being approved."

SEVENTEEN

New Quarters

T he barracks was empty and quiet when I went back to get my stuff. I realized it had been a couple of months since I last heard the sound of quiet. Even when everyone was asleep, the sound of a hundred or more guys breathing filled the space with a flat, steady white noise.

I put all my gear into my duffel bag in just a few minutes, but the quiet was so delicious after the tension of the past few hours, I decided to just sit on my bunk for a while to savor this rare bit of silence.

When I finally got back to the company headquarters, the captain's office door was closed, but the sergeant looked up.

"Take your gear upstairs," he said, "stow it in one of the lockers, and pick out a bunk. Starting tomorrow morning, you no longer go to formation. You report directly down here. That's your desk," he said, pointing to a massive wooden desk and an ancient typewriter that may have been even older than the building itself.

I had assumed I would be the only one using the upstairs space, so I was surprised when I walked into the room and saw that four of the dozen or so beds had already been made—two in one corner and two in the opposite corner. They were as far apart as possible in the limited space.

Clearly, I was an intruder on a yet unknown social structure.

I picked a bunk roughly equidistant from both pairs and moved my things into the nearest locker. Then I sat down and waited for the other residents of the room to show up.

Eventually, I heard a couple of voices engaged in lively conversation moving up the stairs. The conversation ended abruptly when they reached the top of the stairs and realized they were not alone.

After an awkward silence, one of the pair asked the obvious question that managed to combine curiosity, suspicion, and accusation: "Who are you and what are you doing in our room?"

I noticed there was no unit patch or rank on their uniforms, so I could tell that they were trainees and not cadre, so I was less suspicious of them than they appeared to be of me.

I told them my name, where I was from and how I had been assigned to the room by Captain Douglas after I had told him that I was a conscientious objector.

Their reaction to that information puzzled me: they grinned as if they were sharing an inside joke.

"That makes three of us," one of the pair explained.

They were college graduates from East Coast schools who met at Fort Dix and became friends and conscientious objectors at the same time. They informed Captain Douglas of their beliefs separately and had already completed their paperwork requesting they be reclassified and released from the Army.

"Douglas must have gone nuts when you showed up," one of them said.

"Well, it probably explains why he was so angry when I talked to him this afternoon," I said.

"Oh, he was pissed long before that. I'm sure he decided that having two COs in the same unit would ruin his Army career... and that's before you add these two clowns to the mix," he said, gesturing toward the other two made beds across the room.

The two remaining residents of this special quarters for misfits had become legends among the current crop of trainees. The story was that when Martin Luther King, Jr. was assassinated in early April, these two young African-American draftees went AWOL because they "didn't want to miss all the fun" of the anticipated Newark riots.

When things quieted down, they came back to Fort Dix on their own and were assigned to this room while they waited to face their court-martial. The rumor was they never left the post again but could never be found by the Military Police, even though they were reportedly sighted somewhere on the post nearly every day.

I have my doubts about how much—if any—of this tale was true since I never actually met them, but like all stories where the underdog overcomes the odds and beats the system, people want to believe it was possible and the story got repeated and continued to grow.

On the other hand, I was excited about the prospect of getting to know the other two COs. I thought that finally there would be someone I could talk to, but that didn't happen either. They were assigned a variety of menial tasks elsewhere on the post every day, and they kept to themselves when they were not working.

I was disappointed, but their reluctance to open up with others was understandable. Despite being surrounded by people who disagreed with them and were eager to see them fail, they had taken an unpopular stand together. As a result, they regarded others—including me—with caution bordering on distrust.

Now even though I was in a much smaller group, I was still alone when confronted with the daily challenges of a conscientious objector in the Army.

EIGHTEEN
New Role

After the turmoil of the previous day, I had no idea what to expect when I reported to the headquarters office after breakfast.

"Reported" makes it sound like a bigger deal than it was. The sergeant appeared to be the only one in the office, but the door to Captain Douglas's office was almost always closed, so I never knew if he was there or not. Captain Douglas was the commanding officer, but like virtually every unit in the Army, it was the sergeants who ran the show.

On that first morning, I simply walked in and said "Good morning, sergeant."

He looked up to acknowledge my existence, but with a small wordless wave, he let me know that he was on the phone and not to be interrupted.

I sat down at the desk I had been assigned to and waited.

After a few minutes, he hung up, put his now-completed project aside, and with another wave, signaled me to come over to his desk.

"Starting now," he said, "you have only one job. That's to complete your application for a change of status and release from the Army. When the company clerk gets in, he will provide all the necessary materials and instructions to get you started. He will also answer any questions you have. All your future communication should be through him."

The company clerk was the only other person on the office staff. He and the sergeant were polar opposites. The sergeant was a serious, by-the-book career non-commissioned officer (NCO). The company clerk was a young, very skinny, and very mouthy specialist 4. His language was colorful, but crude. He had a favorite all-purpose phrase that he used at least once in nearly every conversation: "Well, kiss my dick."

With a change of the inflection and emphasis, "kiss my dick" was an expression of surprise, agreement, anger, or even a question.

When the company clerk arrived, he spoke briefly with the sergeant and then came to my desk to give me my orientation. He handed me a printed copy of the regulation and plopped a ream of white bond paper, a package of carbon paper, and a stack of yellow second sheets on my desk.

"Here," he said. "You need to submit your original and a copy of everything." And that was the full extent of my instructions. The entire process was completed in less than five minutes.

After that exchange, he rarely spoke to me unless he wanted me to run an errand for him.

I was not about to submit anything without keeping a copy for my own records, and since I was determined to produce an error-free document, correcting mistakes on the original and two carbons slowed my progress considerably.

The first part of my request was detailed background information that took a little digging to complete. It included a list of every school I attended (seven), every place I had worked (ten), and the address of every place I had lived (ten).

Next was what I would call the essay questions: what was my religious background, what were my current religious beliefs, how would I describe the process of discernment that led me to seek conscientious objector status, and what were my denomination's views on conscientious objection. The final category included letters of support from teachers, pastors, priests, friends, and family members.

I felt the essay questions were extremely important because they offered an opportunity to show my sincerity and to demonstrate a well-reasoned statement of belief, so I spent a lot of time writing and editing those statements.

I assumed that the letters of support would also carry a lot of weight, especially letters from teachers and clergy. In general, I was pleased and grateful for the letters that I received, especially the three from clergy, including Chaplain Edward Sterling from Fort Dix, who I earlier thought would not empathize with a conscientious objector.

However, I was saddened that two long-time friends disagreed with my position, refused to write letters of support, and said they did not want to hear from me again.

I had no control over the interviews with an Army chaplain, a psychiatrist, and an investigating officer. Captain Douglas scheduled my three interviews and based on my experience with the three, I concluded that they were chosen because they would have a hostile attitude toward conscientious objectors.

The most negative was Chaplain David W. Williams. He was a Southern Baptist, the assistant brigade chaplain, and an Airborne Ranger (he had a Screaming Eagles unit patch, the symbol of the 101st Airborne, on his uniform).

His report of the interview contained a number of misstatements:

The first was his claim that the religious principles I was basing my application on "are held and taught by Christendom and are not peculiar to the Episcopal church." Actually, my application included several statements by the Episcopal bishops and the General Convention of the Episcopal Church in the United States that acknowledge the validity of conscientious objection. In fact, they were one of the earliest mainline denominations to do so.

He also claimed that I was not prepared to offer constructive, positive service to my country "as an instrument of the love of which he speaks." However, in my application, I state that if released by the Army, I would perform alternative service designated by my local draft board.

His final complaint was the most ludicrous. It made no sense at all. He said my enlistment was prompted by "financial need," but I actually took a 75 percent pay cut when I joined the Army.

During the interview, Williams said that we need the military and "must fight wars in order to maintain peace in the world."

"And how has that been working out for the last couple of hundred years?" I asked. He ignored my question.

Instead, he claimed that I did not have the right attitude about my responsibilities as a soldier. For example, he said if I was in the artillery and my job was to pull the lanyard that fires a shell, what happened after the shell leaves the barrel is not my responsibility.

And similarly, in the infantry, my job would be to pull the trigger on my rifle. What the bullet did after I pulled the trigger would not be my responsibility either.

I could not believe a Christian minister was telling me that an individual has no responsibility for his or her actions.

He concluded his report of the interview this way:

"I have not been able to convince myself that his position is the result of clear logical thought. In light of this information and convinced of the insincerity of the subject's claim, it is therefore recommended that his application not be granted."

NINETEEN
Setting a Deadline

All I did every day was work on some aspect of my application, so I was surprised that no one ever checked to make sure that was what I was actually doing. That was so atypical of the micro-management I had come to expect from the Army's chain of command system, it made me so uneasy that I decided to set my own deadline.

I arbitrarily decided that I would wrap up the process and submit my application two weeks before the end of the current session of AIT. The essay questions would not be a problem. I had written, revised, and rewritten all of them a number of times, and I figured they were as good as they were going to get.

However, with only ten days before my self-imposed deadline, I did not have as many letters of support as I wanted. I sent another round of slightly more urgent-sounding letters, and I also gave Ami a list of names that I wanted her to call.

That last-ditch effort produced two more letters (and one of the "I don't want to hear from you again" replies from a former friend). It wasn't everything I hoped for, but reviewing the document as a whole, I thought it felt honest and sincere.

On a Friday afternoon, I gave the document to the sergeant and asked him to give it to Captain Douglas.

He looked surprised.

"You're finished?" he said.

"Yes," I said.

And that was the only discussion I had with anyone until the last day of the current session of AIT. All the trainees were receiving their orders (it was rarely good news) and packing up for a two-week leave.

Captain Douglas opened his door and asked me to come into his office. He was upbeat...almost jovial.

"Have a seat," he said.

As I sat down, he opened a desk drawer, took out a brown kraft paper envelope, and slid it across the desk to me.

"Here are your orders," he said.

I was confused.

"What orders?" I asked.

"It's your new assignment. Where you are going next...after your two-week leave which starts today by the way. You have to report to Fort Lewis, Washington, on June 17, and they will be responsible for transporting you to your duty station.

"I'm not sure where that is because your orders just arrived here yesterday, and they have the unit name and a Seattle APO (Army Post Office) address, but since you are going through Fort Lewis in Washington, it could be anywhere from Hawaii to Korea.

"It's a mechanized infantry unit, so there's been some speculation here that it's Korea, but that's really just guessing. Maybe you
can find out more while you are on leave.

"By the way, your original orders called for you to be assigned
to the honor guard at Arlington, but that is a prestige assignment. It's
a privilege to be selected to serve there. I told them in Washington
that you did not deserve such a prestige assignment, so now you have
these new orders."

I finally interrupted his monologue:

"Excuse me, sir, but I think there has been a mistake. According
to AR635-20, once someone declares that they are a conscientious
objector, they are supposed to remain with their current unit until
their change-of-status request is completed, submitted, and approved
or rejected. I have already completed and submitted my request and
I'm waiting for a response."

He pulled a second envelope from the drawer and slid it over
to me.

"Here's your request," he said. "I discussed your case at some
length with the battalion commander. We concluded that since there
is nothing in your file about conscientious objection, it would be
better if your new unit handles this matter."

"Better for who?" I asked. "And what about the five or six weeks
of training I missed?"

"According to your DA-20, you have completed the requirements for AIT and have been assigned an 11B10 MOS (Military
Occupational Specialty code). You're a light weapons infantryman."

Ironically in my DA-20 file that he cited, he rated my conduct and my efficiency as "excellent."

I had missed more than a month of training so there is no way I could have completed all the requirements for AIT. He had submitted a falsified report.

"That's all," he said. "You can go. I suggest you go home and get your affairs in order and report to Fort Lewis in a couple of weeks."

I just sat there in a daze.

"That will be all," he repeated.

I stood, gave him a perfunctory salute, and headed upstairs to get my stuff.

I opened my orders and saw that my ultimate destination was 1st Battalion (Mechanized), 47th Infantry, APO Seattle 98731. There was no clue as to where that actually was, and I soon learned it was next to impossible to find a source for that information.

First, I called my wife in Kansas City and told her the surprising news. She had a lot of questions, but I had very few answers.

Next, I called my Aunt Betty in New York City and asked if she could help me get an airline ticket and, if necessary, let me spend the night in her apartment. She said "yes" to both.

I had an hour or so before the next bus to New York City, so I went looking for someone who might be able to tell me the location of APO Seattle 98731.

No one knew for sure, but Chaplain Sterling offered the most encouraging opinion: "I don't know where this is, but I don't think it's Vietnam. Most of the Vietnam APO addresses I'm familiar with are San Francisco."

With that bit of optimism to hang on to, I hurried to catch the bus to New York.

TWENTY

Goin' to Kansas City

I was going home for two weeks. The news was so sudden and totally unexpected that I barely had time to cram all my stuff into my Army duffel bag and catch a late bus to Manhattan.

The seat right behind the bus driver was open, so I took it.

The sight of the main gate of Fort Dix fading in the distance in the driver's big rearview mirror probably should have made me cheer—or at least smile—because I would never have to return to this place, but the thought of how I got here troubled me.

I was going home because Captain Douglas, my commanding officer—the man who questioned the sincerity of my faith, my courage, and my honesty—had falsified my training records, failed to submit my documents as required by Army regulations, and violated proper procedures by processing orders for my reassignment. Although I had no clue that this was going to happen, it bothered me to have been involved in something so obviously dishonest.

I had to keep reminding myself that there was a positive side to what had happened. I would be home, and even though my visit was only for a few days, it was something to look forward to.

By the time I got to New York, it was too late to catch the last flight to Kansas City, but my aunt did her best to put my thoughts of Captain Douglas aside by taking me to our favorite restaurant in Greenwich Village for dinner.

The next morning, I was eagerly looking forward to being home for a couple of weeks, but once I was actually in Kansas City, I realized it no longer felt like home.

When I arrived in early June 1968, the city was still dealing with the aftereffects of the riot following the assassination of Martin Luther King two months earlier. Violence had erupted when police used tear gas to disperse a crowd of student protesters that had gathered outside City Hall. The resulting riot was one of the largest and most destructive in the U.S. Five people were killed and more than twenty were arrested.

The violence was short-lived, but the impact of the riot on attitudes about the Vietnam War, race relations, and political unrest in an already tumultuous election year had a lasting impact on the city.

My phone conversations with Ami or my parents had contained very little news from their world. There seemed to have been a concerted effort to avoid giving me any bad news, so I was unprepared for all the changes that had occurred in the four months I was at Fort Dix.

Finding a place for Ami to live while I was in the Army had been a major concern for us, so we had been relieved when my folks came up with the "ideal solution." Ami moved into my parents' house. She lived upstairs with her own bedroom, bathroom, and a walk-in closet. We tried to convince ourselves that this was going to be just like having her own apartment—except in reality, it was not at all like having her own apartment. It didn't take long for the "ideal solution" to collapse. Looking back, we all probably knew the arrangement was doomed even before it started. My mother and Ami simply didn't like each other. Sometimes, they seemed to be in a contest to see who could be the most stubborn. I think it was probably a tie.

My mother complained that Ami didn't respect the fact that she was a guest in their house. Ami, on the other hand, complained that my mother did not respect her privacy and allow her to come and go as she pleased.

Within a month, she was looking for a new place to stay. She found a furnished apartment over a garage behind a house just a few blocks from our old apartment on the Missouri side of the state line. She talked about it like it was perfect for her, but I thought it was small and cramped. The furniture was old and worn. Nothing in the place was ours, so in my two weeks there, I never felt comfortable.

We had a fairly new car—a Morris Minor that was a little more than a year old—but Ami complained that she always had a "practical car" that somebody else had picked out for her, so she bought a ten-year-old Triumph TR-3 sports car. It was in terrible shape and constantly needed repairs. I never figured out where she got the money, because she had the Morris, too.

She had recently taken on two part-time jobs—waiting tables at a restaurant in the Country Club Plaza shopping center and cashier/clerk at a Pier One Imports store in a Kansas City suburb.

When I asked her about work, she made it clear she hated both jobs, and based on her work history, I figured she would be looking again soon.

She also claimed to have had an affair, but had ended it before I came home. She did not identify the man involved other than to say he was the assistant manager at a retail store in one of the Kansas suburbs and owned a sports car. ("Just a coincidence," she claimed.)

Ami now had her own place, her sports car, her jobs, and her "coincidence." In short, she had her own life and my connection to it was virtually nonexistent.

Of course, I had been in my own separate world for four months, and even though we talked about it often, I was the one who had to live it every day.

There was more pulling us apart than there was keeping us together, but we both felt this was not a time to walk away from our marriage. Sometime down the road, there would be an opportunity for us to resume our *real* life. We could make the hard choices then.

I had my twenty-fourth birthday while I was in Kansas City, but I didn't feel like there was anything worth celebrating, and when the actual day arrived, any thought of trying to make the day festive had vanished.

I got up early that day and walked two blocks over to the Katz Drug Store to get toothpaste. The store was almost empty, but somewhere in the store, the volume was cranked up on a radio. The station was broadcasting the detail of the murder of Robert Kennedy the night before shortly after learning that he had won the California Democratic Presidential Primary.

I went back to Ami's apartment and woke her up to tell her the news. Once I had told her all that I had heard on the radio, there didn't seem to be anything else to say. I went out to buy a morning paper, even though I knew it would be too early to have any news of the killing. Ami had made a pot of coffee, and we sat in the quiet and read all the other news that no longer seemed to have any importance.

The two weeks went by quickly, and I boarded a flight to Seattle and Fort Lewis. My friends were confused when I told them where they could send me mail, but I couldn't tell them where it was. It didn't make any sense to me either.

When my plane took off, we climbed quickly into the low-hanging clouds and I couldn't see the ground until we started down to land in Seattle. It didn't seem real. I was in a plane filled with strangers and I had no idea no idea where I was going.

I felt like I had walked into a metaphor.

TWENTY-ONE
Fort Lewis

F ort Lewis, just south of Tacoma, Washington, was my next stop. As the Army half of a U.S. joint military operation with McChord Air Force Base, Fort Lewis was a very busy place in the late 1960s. More than 300,000 American soldiers went through Basic Training there, and most were sent to Vietnam. The joint operation was also the point of embarkation for thousands more who completed Basic Training at other posts.

I had no idea what the procedure was, but I decided that before they put me on another plane, I would confront the first officer I saw, describe my situation, and explain why I should remain at Fort Lewis until my CO request was handled. I did not know if I would get more than one shot at making my case, so I wrote out a brief speech and memorized it.

I never got to use it.

Like just about everything that happens in the Army, I started the day at the back of a line. Sitting at a table at the headwaters of the line was a very bored-looking sergeant who performed a sort of triage of this day's mélange of tomorrow's forgotten faces.

I handed my orders to him. He glanced at the first page and handed it all right back to me along with a map of Fort Lewis.

"Everyone going to Alaska has to report to the transportation office first," he said as he took out a marker and circled two areas on the map.

"Right now, you're here," he said, indicating one of the two circles.

"The transportation office is right over there," he said, pointing at the second circle. "It's a short walk. Just look for the signs."

As he leaned to one side and called out "Next" to the guy behind me in line, I realized that was all the explanation I was going to get from him.

Alaska? My head was spinning. Was that really where I was headed? Leaving the reception area, I was again just another faceless number, one of a few hundred others that today would be checked off one list and added to another by a bored sergeant.

It only took a few minutes to find the transportation office. When I opened the door and walked in, it was like entering a different world. The office was staffed by a fresh-faced second lieutenant, a couple of sergeants, and three or four spec 4s. They all greeted me as if I was an old friend.

One of the sergeants explained that their primary job was to get a few hundred troops on planes to 'Nam every day. It was repetitive, boring, and often depressing work. About 99 percent of soldiers who came to Fort Lewis from elsewhere were gone in less than forty-eight hours.

However, for the handful of soldiers headed to Alaska, it was a different story. The transportation office had to arrange for us to fly on a commercial airline using unsold seats. Rarely more than six or seven soldiers at a time were headed north, and empty seats were hard to come by, so Alaska-bound troops could spend a week or more waiting for a flight. And when a seat did become available, the staff needed to make sure they didn't lose it. We were instructed not to go to the mandatory morning roll call or any other formation.

"If you go to any formation at all," I was told, "you could end up spending all day on KP or some equally unpleasant work detail, and it would be difficult for us to find you if a flight became available."

So every morning, I went directly to the transportation office with my duffel bag and other belongings. After dinner, I returned to a transitional barracks that was filled with a few hundred bunks. I stowed my gear under a bed and tried to get some sleep.

One night I became aware of a team of soldiers with flashlights moving around the room. They would check the name on the duffel bag under a bed, wake the sleeping soldier, identify him by name, and tell him to get up because his name was on their KP list.

I hoped they would get all of the "volunteers" they needed before they got to me, but eventually, I saw them shining their lights under my bed.

"Parkinson?" one of them said. "Get all your gear and come with us. Your name is on our list for KP."

I was sure there was no list, but I couldn't ignore a direct order or accuse them of lying.

Instead, I said, "I can't. I'm flying to Alaska in the morning."

They obviously were not accustomed to having someone ignore their order. They stood silently for a minute, and one of them finally spoke up:

"Are you sure?" he said.

I delivered a lengthy and detailed explanation and gave them the lieutenant's name and urged them to call him to confirm it.

They decided it was easier to wake up someone else rather than to continue to argue with me, so they moved on.

Later, I told my story to the transportation guys, and they got a good laugh over it.

"I'm glad I was able to think that quickly," I said. "But I feel sorry for the guy who is probably going to 'Nam and had to spend his last day in the States on pots and pans duty."

The transportation office felt more like a social club than the Army. There were card games, board games, magazines and books, a TV set, and a ping pong table. The staff was always eager to join us.

At meal time, we found ourselves talking about our families, what we did before the Army, and what we would do after.

The wives of the two senior NCOs had followed their husbands to the Seattle area, and on my second day there, one of them made a chocolate cake for her husband's birthday and brought it to the office for lunch. Not to be outdone, the next day, the other spouse made brownies.

When I arrived at Fort Lewis, there were already a couple of guys waiting for a flight to Alaska, and our group had grown to eight by the time we left. Three got off in Anchorage, and the rest of us continued to Fairbanks.

We were booked on an Alaska Airlines flight. It was unlike any plane I had ever been on before. The interior of the Boeing 727 had been completely redecorated as part of the airline's "Gold Nugget Days" promotion. The walls were covered with deep red flocked wallpaper, and there was ball fringe on the bottom of the overhead luggage storage compartments. The flight attendants were dressed as saloon girls with net opera hose.

Even the in-flight announcements fit the theme. They were written in the style of Robert Service's epic Yukon poems like "The Cremation of Sam McGee" and "The Shooting of Dan McGrew," and they were recorded by professional actors.

The only fragment I can recall is: "We're setting down in Fairbanks town…"

The final touch was free beer for the duration of the flight. That was clearly the most popular feature of Gold Nugget Days with the soldiers on board. Perhaps it was a little too popular with some. One of our group members was so drunk, he could not figure out how to unlock the door of the lavatory to get out and return to his seat. A flight attendant had to unlock the door from outside to let him out.

A bus from Fort Wainwright met us at the Fairbanks airport and took us to the base for "inprocessing."

TWENTY-TWO

C Company...Just Passing Through

When I arrived at Fort Wainwright, Alaska, I was assigned to C Company, 1st Battalion, 47th Infantry (Mechanized). As I recall, it was a Friday afternoon when I finally got to the C Company barracks where I met the company clerk. I liked him immediately. He took me up to the second floor to get a bunk and a locker.

He told me that the other guy in the cubicle was also fairly new to C Company.

"I really don't know him yet," the company clerk said, "but he has a reputation as a troublemaker. The story I heard is that he was in the 82nd Airborne, but when the entire Division was reassigned to Vietnam, he was one of two men who the commanding general refused to take with them."

He was a scary-looking dude. He was missing a large chunk of one ear. The other guy who was left behind by the 82nd was the one who bit it off, but they both claimed they were buddies.

They would get together with a couple of other guys every night to play cards in our cubicle, and they used my bed as their table… even when I was already in it.

The company clerk apologized for assigning me to a situation he knew would probably be uncomfortable.

"I should be able to move you in a week or so," he said, "But if there are any serious problems before then, let me know."

I only had to put up with this nightmare for three nights, but that was more than enough.

After stowing my stuff in my locker, the company clerk showed me how to get to the EM Club (Enlisted Men's Club) and told me what they offered (beer and bingo and little else).

He told me the easiest way to get into town from the barracks—a short walk to the little-used back gate that led to the Alaska Highway. From there, I could hitch a ride the rest of the way into town—just a couple of miles. It was easy for a soldier to catch a ride into Fairbanks, he reported. There was also free bus service to and from a couple of locations on the base. He had tips on which bars to stay away from and which officers and NCOs to avoid, as well.

Then bad news: on Monday, everyone in C Company would spend the day in the base armory cleaning weapons.

I told him that I could not do that and explained my situation. He had never heard of another case like mine and asked several questions. He said he would let the company commander, a first lieutenant, know about my situation.

"He's not going to be happy about that," he added.

In the meantime, he encouraged me to go into town over the weekend, look around, and have some fun. Which I did.

It was the Summer Solstice and in Fairbanks, where the winters were long, bitterly cold, and dark around-the-clock, twenty-four hours of daylight was well-worth celebrating. I spent a day and a half exploring the town and watching a baseball game between two town teams that started at midnight and was played without lights.

I also found St. Matthew's Episcopal Church, a small but attractive log church with brightly colored, stained glass windows depicting Alaskan scenes.

I went back for Sunday worship and met the priest, Rev. William Warren, who invited me to join his family for Sunday dinner, an invitation that I gladly accepted. The meal was wonderful, and Father Warren and I had the first of several conversations about conscientious objection, the Episcopal Church's position, and our personal beliefs.

Afterwards as I headed back to the barracks, I felt I had found a friend and an ally in the company clerk, but my good mood was short-lived. One of the men who also bunked on the second floor introduced himself, but then gave me some terrible news: the company clerk and another soldier had been killed late Saturday night in an accident on the highway just outside the back gate. No one knew the details, but these sudden deaths affected everyone in the company.

On Monday as everyone in C Company was preparing to go to the armory, I told our platoon leader that I needed to see the company commander. He said that was not possible, but I dug my heels in and refused to go with the rest of the company. He eventually talked to the senior NCO who talked to the commanding officer and after a lengthy wait, I got to tell my story.

I don't know how much—if anything—the company commander knew about my situation before our brief meeting, but he was clearly in no mood to deal with it. He already had enough problems on his plate. Unlike Captain Douglas, however, he did not try to argue or threaten me. He just wanted time.

"Couldn't you just go with the rest of the company today and we can talk about your situation later?" he asked.

When I turned him down and explained why, he decided to push the problem upstairs.

"You're going to have to deal with Colonel Colonna," he said. "He's strictly by the book and tough. You may wish you had gone with the rest of the company today."

He probably intended that to be a threat, but he just sounded exasperated. I had told my story many times since my first effort with Captain Douglas at Fort Dix. I was more comfortable now, and hopefully, my explanation was more polished and more convincing, but that didn't change the dynamic of this situation. I would be dealing with a senior officer. I was the newest and lowest-ranking soldier in his command, someone he knew nothing about and I was presenting a problem that no one else was willing to tackle. I didn't hold out any hope that this time the outcome would be any different.

TWENTY-THREE

Lieutenant Colonel Gary S. Colonna

T he company commander was right about one thing: Lieutenant Colonel Gary S. Colonna was a by-the-book, no-nonsense senior Army officer. He took his job seriously with a quiet intensity that was intimidating to someone dealing with him for the first time.

As I recall, his office was rather stark. A large military issue metal desk dominated the room. When Colonel Colonna was at his desk, he was clearly in charge of the space, even if others in the room outranked him.

He was smart, perceptive, decisive, and a good listener. He believed a good leader is someone who leads by example. His uniform was always clean and wrinkle-free, even when we were in the field.

His first question to me was, "Why are you here? Not just 'why are you in Alaska,' but why are you here in my office today?"

I told him that I had just arrived in Alaska and had been assigned to C Company.

"Today, the company is spending the entire day at the base armory cleaning weapons, and as a conscientious objector, I cannot do that," I explained.

He did not appear surprised by my claim of conscientious objection, but he probed deeper: Was I just opposed to the war in Vietnam or all wars? How and when did I become a conscientious objector? By now I had told that story several times, but he appeared to want to hear everything, so I told it with more detail than usual.

Then he asked to see the request I had written back at Fort Dix. He looked carefully at each page. At one point, he stopped, looked up from the stack of papers, and smiled.

"I thought I recognized you," he said. "You were at St. Matthew's yesterday, weren't you? Was that the first time you were there?"

"Yes, sir. I was there yesterday. It was my first visit, because I just got to Alaska on Friday."

"Most Sundays I ring the call-to-worship bell at St. Matthew's," he said. "You must have walked right by me. Next time, be sure to say hello."

As we continued to talk, I could sense that he was getting angry, but for once, it was not directed at me.

"You shouldn't be in a line company," he said curtly. "You shouldn't be here at all. Your CO at Fort Dix—what's his name? Whatever. He should have had the courage to deal with this himself instead of passing it off on someone else. He doesn't deserve to be an officer in the United States Army!"

He paused for a moment, considering his options, and then summoned the sergeant seated outside his office.

"Sergeant Graves! Can you step in here for a minute?"

When Sgt. Graves appeared in the doorway, Colonel Colonna said, "Sgt. Graves, this is Private Parkinson. Do you think we could find a bunk for him at Headquarters Company? I want him to start working up here as soon as possible. He can use the empty storage room across the hall. Once it's straightened up, it should work as a decent office."

Sgt. Graves, a career NCO, seemed to know in broad strokes what the colonel wanted him to do. He also knew that it would serve no useful purpose for him to ask questions that the colonel had not yet considered, like "What is this man going to do here?" or "Where are we going to put him on the org chart?" So, he simply said, "Yes, sir." Besides, Graves knew that eventually he would be the one to answer the unasked questions.

It was agreed that Sgt. Graves would contact Lieutenant Zarro, the commanding officer of Headquarters Company, and arrange for my transfer. I was instructed to gather all my gear and report to Zarro.

Colonel Colonna offered a final word of advice: "Don't tell any Zorro jokes. He says he has heard them all and doesn't think any of them are funny. I'll see you back here bright and early tomorrow morning."

The three of us exchanged salutes and I headed back to C Company.

I couldn't believe what had just happened. Someone in a position of authority had listened to me, offered support, and taken action. I realized that, ultimately, it was still very unlikely that my request would ever be approved, but this was the first positive thing to happen since I got off the bus at Fort Dix. I had expected my meeting with Colonel Colonna would be another episode like my confrontation with Captain Douglas, so I decided to just enjoy the moment while it lasted.

TWENTY-FOUR

Headquarters Company

1st Battalion (Mechanized), 47th Infantry Headquarters Company was one of four companies that made up the 1st Battalion. Companies A, B, and C were mostly light weapons infantrymen. Foot soldiers.

Headquarters Company maintained and operated most of the battalion vehicles, primarily Armored Personnel Carriers (APCs) that provided transport for troops and the battalion staff during maneuvers.

Headquarters Company was in a state of confusion when I arrived.

Lieutenant John Zarro had been the commanding officer for less than a month, and he was eager to establish a reputation as an officer to be reckoned with. He had immediately ordered a thorough inspection of the barracks, the motor pool, and every soldier's gear. That was probably too ambitious for a new commanding officer's first official action, especially since he was conducting the inspection himself, but he was determined to show everyone he was in charge.

It was the first day of the inspection when I arrived, and Lt. Zarro did not have time to deal with the bureaucratic details of my transfer. I was turned over to Spec 4 Joe Arnett, the unit's new company clerk. Like me, Arnett was a college graduate who had dropped out of the OCS program while he was in Basic Training and now found himself in Alaska.

Arnett had been assigned to Sergeant Dewey Phillips' platoon simply because, at the time, there was a bed available on the third floor where the rest of the platoon bunked.

The other bunk in Arnett's cubicle was now empty, so I moved in and we became friends. Arnett got married in July, and he and his wife moved into an apartment off the base, so I saw him less frequently after that.

Sgt. Phillips did not appear to know anything about maintaining or operating a military vehicle, but for some reason, he had been put in charge of a platoon of drivers and their vehicles.

The drivers were a close-knit unit. Most of them had been together for a year or more. They usually ate together, went to town together, and hung out in the same bars. As the new kid on the block, I got the same treatment as a new kidney gets in an organ transplant: the body tries to reject the foreign object. It very quickly became obvious to me that it would be difficult—if not impossible—for me to become a welcome part of this group.

To begin with, our jobs were totally different. Every morning we split up: I reported to Battalion Headquarters, and everyone else went to the motor pool. At the end of the day, their uniforms were often covered with dirt and grease, while mine was still clean. It was no secret that some of the drivers resented the fact that I had what they considered to be a cushy job. They frequently complained to one another, but they just ignored me.

Sgt. Phillips was a loner, so in the first couple of weeks after Arnett moved out, he surprised me and everyone else when he stopped by my cubicle "to see how I was getting along." He would sit down on the empty bunk and begin a rambling conversation. It was more monologue than conversation, because he was not interested in anything I had to say. Phillips just wanted to talk. He needed someone to listen to his sad story. Over time, I learned much more about him than I really wanted to know.

Phillips was a sergeant, but he confided with some pride that he had been promoted to Staff Sergeant twice. However, according to Philips, both times when he was promoted, his superior "had it in for him," and he was demoted. His drivers, however, suggested it was Phillips' fondness for alcohol rather than a vindictive superior that was responsible for the demotions.

In one of our "conversations," he did admit that for relaxation, he would go to the NCO Club where drinks were cheap.

"I like a good drink every now and then," he said, "but that's gotten me in trouble more than once," he said. "That's why I don't go into town," he admitted. "I've been here for nearly two years and that's how many times I've been to town: two."

One morning, Phillips decided it would be a good idea to clear up any confusion in the platoon about my status. He called a meeting of the platoon that included everyone except me.

His explanations usually made a situation more confusing, and this was no exception. He told them I was a conscientious objector so I would not to be assigned to guard duty or any other activity that required me to use a weapon.

"But that does not mean it's OK to give him a hard time. Parkinson should be treated just like any other soldier. I don't want to hear about him being the target of any harassment."

When he finished his lecture, he asked if there were any questions.

One hand shot up.

"Yes. What's your question?" he said.

"What's a conscientious objector?" the soldier asked.

The questioner was Matthews, a smart ass who enjoyed giving Phillips a hard time, but Phillips missed the sarcasm and assumed the question was sincere, so he began an even longer and more confusing explanation.

Rather than clearing things up, it gave Matthews an idea. Phillips' speech made me out to be some kind of weirdo, and after a Friday night spent visiting the bars on Second Avenue in downtown Fairbanks, Matthews introduced a new sport back in the barracks: "Let's see who can get this hippie peacenik to fight."

It was typical drunken harassment. Standing nose-to-nose, he unleashed a string of tough-guy insults, trying to goad me into a fight. He put his hands on my chest and pushed me backwards until I was pinned against the lockers.

"I'm not going to fight you," I said.

That just made him madder, and he began screaming at me.

When I refused to hit him, it took all the fun out of the game. The other drivers who had gathered to watch the fight, started to slip away.

"Come on, Matthews. Give it up. You're just embarrassing yourself," Cappeletti, Lt. Col. Colonna's driver, said.

Everyone returned to their cubicles and things quieted down. Later that night, almost everyone was asleep when Cappeletti came back into my cubicle and asked if I was going to report Matthews.

"Did he send you in here to find that out?" I asked.

"No," he said. "It's just me trying to keep the peace in the platoon."

"I don't plan to say anything. He's just immature and needed to blow off some steam," I said.

Cappeletti nodded and left.

After that night, I was once again ignored by my peers.

TWENTY-FIVE

My New Job

After breakfast on my first full day in the new company, I walked up to Battalion Headquarters to start my new job, only to discover that officially there was no real job. I found this disconcerting, but I seemed to be the only one who was concerned.

As I later learned, Alaska was such a low priority for manpower, equipment, and other war-making necessities, unit commanders were given considerable leeway in making personnel assignments. They did whatever they needed to do to get by, knowing that the senior command structure would simply look the other way.

Sgt. Graves took the direct approach. He just put me to work. He unlocked the door to a cluttered storage room across the hall from Colonel Colonna's office.

"This is your space," he said. "Or your office or whatever you want to call it. Or it will be yours as soon as it's cleaned up and organized. You can start now."

He left me standing there staring at a room full of miscellaneous stuff, much of which had no apparent use or value. A lot of it was paper—maps, copies of Army and USARAL (United States Army Alaska) regulations, and stacks of various reports involving people and events that no one currently part of the battalion could possibly identify. I spent a couple of weeks throwing away stuff that I was sure no one would miss and organizing the rest of it. The best description of my job at that point would have been "Librarian." According to my personnel file, during my time in Alaska, I was a Light Truck Operator, Light Weapons Infantryman, a Ground Survey Radar Repairman, and Operations and Intelligence Specialist. Of course, I never did any of those things.

However, if anyone ever asked about my position, I was told to say that I was the Battalion S3 Clerk. In the civilian world, S3 would have been called Operations, but the Army chose to develop their own alpha-numeric designations to basic functions rather than use perfectly good words that everyone could understand: Personnel was S1, Intelligence and Security was S2, and Supplies and Logistics was S4.

As my job evolved, S3 Clerk turned out to be a fairly accurate description of what I actually did.

There were only three of us in the S3 group. Second Lieutenant Tom Magnificci was the S3 Officer. Staff Sergeant Warne was the third member of the group. Warne had reportedly been severely wounded in Vietnam and spent nearly a year in Fitzsimmons Army Hospital in Colorado recovering. Everything was serious to Warne, especially having to work alongside a conscientious objector, and he never missed an opportunity to point that out.

Magnificci, on the other hand, was the youngest officer in the unit and full of youthful enthusiasm. There was very little that he took seriously. It was understood that officers only socialized with other officers, but Magnificci ignored that convention and became a casual friend in addition to being my boss. He would come into my office, pull up a chair, and talk about whatever was on his mind—from a new joke he was anxious to share, the war in Vietnam, or George Wallace's Presidential campaign. When he left to return to his own office, he almost always closed by encouraging me to write about absurdities he had observed as an Army officer:

"Parkinson, you need to write a book."

Every six to eight weeks, the battalion took part in training exercises. The S3 group was responsible for all the paperwork. That included the scenario for the maneuvers: who we were allegedly fighting, our objective, and what the unit was supposed to be learning from the activity.

A training exercise was essentially an adult version of a game of "Pretend." We would pack up all of our gear—tents, sleeping bags, Yukon stoves, radios, and rifles (but no ammo)—and head for the boonies where we set up a command post and attempted to neutralize the imaginary foe that was the focus of those maneuvers.

A team of officers from other units served as the referees and official scorers. If we did a good job of pretending, we got a good grade. But if we screwed up, the referees would tell our commanders that a certain number of us were dead. Being dead was an easy role, but it got boring quickly.

Much of my job in preparing for maneuvers was making copies. The photocopiers we take for granted today were not readily available then, so my job required me to make a master for a mimeograph machine and run copies. Getting a clean master was the hard part and running off copies was easy, so the author of each report, list or other document would always ask for five or ten more copies than he really needed. It quickly became clear how easily my office had been filled with trash.

Map boards became my specialty. I mounted topographic maps to cardboard panels so that a large map could be folded up to a manageable size and then I covered the panels with clear sheets of plastic so the user could track troop movements with a grease pencil. For the finishing touch, I used my calligraphy ability to put the unit name, the title of the operation, the date, and the name of the officer on the front.

Old English lettering was everyone's favorite, even though I didn't think it was appropriate for military maps. In fact, it was so popular that when Lt. Magnificci saw his name on the map board, he asked if I could letter a sign for his desk. Magnificci was so proud of his fancy nameplate that he showed it all around, and before I knew what was happening, I had requests from every officer and NCO for a sign for their desk and office door. When I presented one to Sgt. Warne, it marked a change in our relationship. Maybe working with a conscientious objector wasn't such a bad deal after all.

When Colonel Colonna saw the name signs I had created, he decided that we needed a sign for the battalion outside the headquarters building that included the unit's history back to its inception in World War II. He had only two requirements: It had to be the largest unit sign at Fort Wainwright, and it had to be Old English lettering.

TWENTY-SIX

Winter

I arrived in Fairbanks at the peak of summer. The weather was spectacular and the fireweed had just started to bloom, turning the low hills around the city bright red. And there were people outside everywhere. They were eagerly spending the energy they had been saving up while the Alaskan winter kept them inside.

The long-time Alaskans had seen this show before. They knew that the fireweed season for all its flash would soon be followed by another winter. And this year, the fireweed had come early, prompting the old-timers to warn that "it's gonna be a rough one this year." They were right.

For newcomers like me, the horror stories that the long-time residents loved to tell about Alaskan winters sounded like tall tales. True or not, there was nothing I could do about the approaching winter, but at that moment, there were long summer days to be enjoyed.

The weather was just one of many differences that made living in Alaska interesting and challenging.

The Army's response was to publish *Welcome to Alaska*, a booklet that made the modest claim that it "tells you everything you need to know about our 49th state." A lot of effort obviously went into creating it, but they dropped the ball by not printing enough so every new arrival could have his or her own copy.

The booklet included a brief history of Alaska (apparently the Army believes Alaska's history began in 1867 when the United States purchased the territory from Russia).

There was a section on the native population: a map that shows the geographic distribution of the five primary native groups, a discussion about native customs, food, traditions, and terms. It also provides the derogatory terms that refer to native Alaskans along with a strict prohibition from using them.

The practical information about coping with the cold was clearly focused on military applications: how to set up a ten-man tent, camouflage it, and set up a Yukon stove to heat it.

The most comprehensive and most useful section offered tips on how the individual could deal with the cold. "How to avoid frost-bite" was followed by "How to treat frostbite."

There was even advice for anyone who planned to have a car while in Alaska: installing an engine block heater, using frost shields on your windows, using dipstick heaters, adjusting the tire pressure, and switching to light weight engine oil.

I came across a copy of the brochure on my first day at Fort Wainwright. I was in the Personnel office waiting for a clerk to process the paperwork that would officially make me part of USARAL.

I asked the clerk where I could get a copy. He apologized, but informed me they did not have enough copies for everyone, but I could check out a copy from my company library (if it had one), the post library, or the personnel office. But after I was finished at the personnel office, my life got busy and whatever free time I had was spent enjoying the remaining summer. All the worrisome stories about winter were fading away until a supply clerk unexpectedly showed up at my office door.

"Parkinson?" he said.

"Yes?"

"You 're a hard person to find," he said. "I was told you were in C Company, but no one there had ever heard of you. It's no big deal. I just need you to pick up your winter gear. How about tomorrow morning?"

"Sure," I said. The next morning, I stopped by Supply.

The clerk looked surprised when I showed up.

"Didn't you bring anybody with you?" he said. "You're going to need a couple of trips if you are taking everything yourself. What size shoe do you wear?"

"Ten."

He plopped a pair of large, bulbous, white waterproof rubber boots onto the counter. It was the first of several surprises.

"What are those?" I asked.

"The official description is 'Extreme Cold Vapor Barrier Boots, Type II'," he said, "but almost everyone calls them 'Mickey Mouse boots.' They keep your feet warm in temperatures down to minus 60°."

"Sixty below? Does it really get that cold?"

"Nah. It rarely gets below −30°," he said.

I did the math quickly in my head:

"That would be 100° colder than it will be today."

And that was just the beginning of my winter gear. He added an ancient pair of wooden skis, a giant pair of snowshoes, three pieces of white camouflage, a parka with a fur-lined hood, a pair of arctic mittens that looked like oven hot pads that came up to my elbows, leather gloves with two pairs of wool liners, several pairs of wool socks, and an insulated bomber hat with flaps.

By the time he was finished, the counter was filled with gear that was all made for a common purpose: to keep you safe and warm in extreme cold.

The yarns that the old-timers told might have been exaggerated, or in some cases, complete fabrications, but the pile of gear in front of me was a convincing argument that winter in Alaska should not be taken lightly.

TWENTY-SEVEN
Going to Town

I t's no secret why the residents of Fairbanks welcome their few summer months with such enthusiasm. After their long, cold, and dark winters, the city enjoys twenty-four hours of daylight on June 21st every year. But Fairbanks had an additional reason to celebrate the summer in 1968. The previous August, the city suffered through ten straight days of constant rain that produced the worst flood in the city's history. The normally placid Chena River that runs adjacent to First Avenue on the north edge of downtown rose rapidly to sixteen feet above flood stage. Nearly half of the inhabitants were displaced.

When the water subsided, there was very little time to clean up before the first hard freeze and snow storm hit.

In the summer of 1968 when the weather turned warm again, everyone was eager to get outside and make the most of their short summer. Sgt. Phillips' advice to the contrary, I was going to join the good people of Fairbanks whenever possible.

A story about the Tanana Valley State Fair in the *Fairbanks News-Miner*—one of two daily papers that served this city of 18,000—caught my attention. The fair is a ten-day event held just outside

Fairbanks. There are actually two "State Fairs" vying for the right to call themselves "The Official Alaska State Fair." The dispute was resolved by the Governor: The title rotates. In even numbered years, the Tanana Valley State Fair is The Official Alaska State Fair" and in odd numbered years the fair held in Palmer uses that designation.

Both are old-fashioned state fairs featuring competition for biggest or best produce, baked goods, homemade jellies and jams, live entertainment, carnival rides, fireworks, and an arts and crafts show. On a spur of the moment impulse, I decided to do a quick portrait of Bob Dylan and enter it in the show.

It was also an election year, so there were lots of visiting politicians eager to meet and greet, including three politicians who rose to national prominence: Ted Stevens, the longest serving Republican in the U.S. Senate; Wally Hickel, former Governor who became Secretary of the Interiorr; and Ernest Gruening, one of two members of the U.S. Senate who voted against the Gulf of Tonkin Resolution that President Lyndon Johnson used to justify the increased involvement of American combat troops on the ground in Vietnam.

Politics is very personal in Alaska. As Senator Gruening walked around the fairgrounds, he greeted people by name and if they had written to him, he could usually remember the issue that prompted their letter.

He introduced himself to me and asked how I was doing.

"I'm doing fine," I said, "but I'm not an Alaska resident, Senator."

In other words, he didn't need to spend his time with me.

"I figured you're at Fort Wainwright," he said, "so you're still a constituent of mine, regardless of where you're from. Tell me, what do you think of our state fair?"

"I'm enjoying it," I told him, "but today I'm most interested in the arts and crafts exhibit, because I have a painting in the show."

That drew sort of a "wow" look from the Senator.

"Well, good luck, Mr. Parkinson."

We shook hands and went our separate ways.

Of course, I was anxious to find the arts and crafts building and check out the competition. Finding the building was not difficult, but finding my painting of Bob Dylan was more challenging. There were two or three times more pieces on the walls, tables, and floor than the space could comfortably handle. My painting was hung just four inches off the floor.

But there was something else in the display that made me forget about how poorly it was displayed. There were two ribbons hanging on my painting. The blue ribbon said "FIRST PLACE" and the Purple one said "CHAMPION."

My painting also got a one-sentence mention in the *News-Miner's* story about the arts and crafts competition: "Unfortunately, Mr. Parkinson's painting was poorly displayed."

When the fair closed, I headed back to the fairgrounds to reclaim my prize-winning painting. On the way, I ran into John Polodna. He was at Fort Dix at the same time I was. We had talked a few times, but hardly enough to be considered close friends. However, seeing a familiar face in an unfamiliar place was a pleasant surprise, so I asked John if he would like to join me on my trek to the fairgrounds, and he enthusiastically agreed. That was the beginning of a friendship that has lasted for more than half a century.

At the time, John was the personal Jeep driver for, O. G. Garrett, a full-bird Colonel and the brigade commander. When we discovered that John and all the other the enlisted men in Col. Garrett's staff had their bunks and lockers on the second floor of the building where my office was located, we couldn't believe that our paths had not crossed earlier. We got together frequently after that.

That changed when General John C. Bennett was named the new Post Commandant for Fort Wainwright. He wanted to choose his own driver. John applied, and after he got the job, he had to move across the post so he could be closer to the general's office. Getting together was more difficult, but now John had his own room with a door that locked and a private bathroom. For a Spec 4, that was unheard of luxury.

TWENTY-EIGHT
Staying Busy

I don't think anyone knew what to expect when I was assigned to battalion headquarters, least of all me. There was no job description or clearly defined role. That led a number of people to incorrectly assume that I didn't have enough to do and they attempted to correct that perception.

That's how I ended up with a hodgepodge of tasks, many of them totally unrelated to the Army, like painting the names and logos of the civilian companies and merchants that sponsored Brigade First Sergeant Workman's competition snowmobile for the Iron Dog Race from Nome to Anchorage. If he had used a civilian sign painter, the job probably would have cost him a couple of hundred dollars. I got nothing.

On maneuvers, I was Colonel Colonna's unofficial stand-in, answering his calls on the radio when he was busy or just didn't want to be bothered. I even had my own code name: "Grey Fox X-ray." The Colonel was "Grey Fox Leader."

Later in the summer when we were preparing for a major joint maneuver involving the entire post and the Illinois Air National Guard, Colonel Colonna mentioned that he had seen me carrying around a "professional-looking camera" and he wondered if I would take some pictures of the exercise.

"This is a big deal," he said. "So, all the media guys will be sticking close to the generals and we will be ignored."

I agreed to do it and the pictures turned out well. Lt. Col. Colonna was pleased…especially when the post paper ran a couple of them. Sergeant Wakefield, the editor of the paper, was also pleased. He was the paper's only photographer, so he was happy to have another source for photos.

From then on, my "weapon of choice" was a 35-mm camera. I not only took pictures of battalion activities. I also became an unofficial part-time photographer and writer for the paper.

Colonel Colonna noticed my byline in the paper, so he asked me about my major in college. When I reminded him that I was a journalism major, he said he would like my help with some occasional writing projects.

"It's a tradition that when an officer leaves his first assignment here—especially if he's going from here to Vietnam—I submit his name for the Army Commendation Medal. I would appreciate your help writing those recommendations. There aren't a lot of them. One, maybe two every month or so," he added.

He showed me a copy of the one-page nomination form and a sample of an Officer's Efficiency Report (OER) that ranks an officer in relation to his peers.

"This is all the information you will need," he said.

I agreed to help.

"Good," he said, "because I have one today."

The first one was easy. The nominee's OER was glowing. I just cleaned it up a bit and was getting ready to type it when I noticed a line at the bottom of the form: "If you need more space, attach a second page."

That sounded like a hint to me. If this guy is so great, how is it possible to sum up all his accomplishments in less than half a page?

I decided that would be my model. I would make sure that all of my submissions would require a second page.

That seemed to work. I had a 100 percent success rate, and I was getting a little cocky. Then the Colonel gave me a clunker. He was ranked eighteenth out of eighteen officers. His OER was decidedly negative. I stretched and padded his story until it barely creeped over to the second page. And I struggled to find synonyms that were more upbeat than those in his evaluation.

Still, I was surprised when he was actually awarded a medal. I concluded that it wasn't my brilliant obfuscation that carried the day. It seemed more likely that if a senior officer nominated someone, the nomination itself virtually assured that a medal would be awarded. Ever since then, whenever I see a highly decorated general in his formal uniform, I wonder how many of the ribbons on his chest had a second page in the nomination write-up.

My very first assignment at this makeshift job had been to clean up and organize the stuff in the space that would become my office. In the process, I uncovered a whole library of official Army regulations. Most of them were U.S. Army regulations, but there were also some Department of Defense (DOD) and USARAL policies and regulations. Getting rid of the outdated and duplicate copies turned out to be more complicated than I expected, but eventually, I was able to announce the opening of the S3 Collection of Regulations and Policies (S3-CRAP), and I was surprised to discover that occasionally it was a useful source of information for me because most career officers and NCOs had an inflated and unrealistic view of their knowledge about what the regulations really say.

The so-called "Moustache Regulation" was an excellent example of this trait. Every new soldier had to be clean shaven when his military ID photo was taken during Basic Training. Later, if the soldier wanted to grow a moustache, some by-the-book officer or NCO would invariably tell him he can only grow a moustache if his ID photo shows him with a moustache. That's a classic Catch-22. Except it's not true.

It was the Army's way of preventing someone from growing a moustache without actually prohibiting it.

There is no such regulation, but you can't convince the career guy that he is wrong. I know, because someone was always giving me a hard time about my moustache. In Alaska, however, I was able to show him a copy of the actual USARAL Moustache Regulation that states a moustache is not considered a distinguishing feature for purposes of identification.

In other words, you can have a moustache regardless of what your ID photo looks like. I took smug pleasure in showing the by-the-book guys that they didn't really know what was in the book, but I always had to remind myself not to overdo it, because subjecting a higher-ranking soldier to humiliation has never been a good career move. The other regulation that I always had with me was AR635-20

Personnel Separation—Conscientious Objection. Although it was crucial to my future, I rarely had to refer to it because there were very few who had even heard of it, so they were reluctant to discuss it. However, there was one issue that puzzled nearly everyone. After I explained the requirements spelled out in the regulation, they would say "But you enlisted?"

I was always surprised by the level of interest in my work. I didn't consider anything I did in while I was in the Army to be particularly remarkable, but over time, I realized that I was simply a curiosity. I had a one-of-a-kind job. I was in an infantry unit, but did not carry a weapon. I was a conscientious objector, but many soldiers did not know what that was or why I was in the Army at all.

TWENTY-NINE
Hiding in Plain Sight

When I got up in the morning, I put on a uniform and went to work where I would be surrounded by many more people—almost always men—in the same uniform. It reminded me of the sign I had seen in the barracks at Fort Dix: "War is our business and business is good."

I was a conscientious objector, so no one at Fort Wainwright had ever asked me to carry or use a weapon, but that did not change the fact that I was working for a bunch of people in the war business.

The war was not being waged in Fairbanks where I was, but I had to ask myself if I was doing anything—even indirectly—to assist the management of violence in Vietnam.

As James Mattis, a retired general and former Secretary of Defense put it: "In an organization, you become complicit in what that organization is doing."

I was uncomfortable being seen in a uniform—especially when I was off the post—because it labeled me as someone who was in the war business. Whenever possible, I got into my civvies, left the post, and spent as much time as possible some place that did not have any connection to the military.

One of my favorite places to hide out was the campus of the University of Alaska perched on a hill in College, Alaska, about four miles from downtown Fairbanks. Just getting there was usually a pleasant escape. If the weather was nice and I had the entire day ahead of me, I would walk there. The houses along the quiet back roads were modest and frequently in need of repairs. If anyone was outside, they always greeted me warmly. A few of the homes had kennels along the road where the owners kept their sled dog teams.

Most days, I did not have time to make the four-mile trek and I would hitchhike. The driver often assumed I was a college student, and they were eager to share stories with a stranger.

I usually took a book with me to read and a notebook so I could write letters. Some days, I would stretch out in the grassy area at the base of the twenty-foot-tall totem pole that was one of the university's landmarks. Other times, I chose one of the library's comfy chairs where I would often fall asleep.

Sunday morning was reserved for Saint Matthew's Church, the beautiful little log church that was perched on the banks of the Chena River, a short walk from downtown Fairbanks. Behind the church was a large white house that served as a residential alcohol treatment facility for native Alaskans that was operated by the church.

I was surprised to learn that Alaska was a Mission District of the Episcopal Church of America, which I guess made Father Warren a missionary and me a heathen.

When soldiers started talking about busting loose or getting away from military life, they were usually talking about hitting the bar scene. In Fairbanks in 1968, the bar scene was Second Avenue downtown. There was something for just about every interest or taste to choose from. The Gold Rush Saloon was a "theme bar" where everything tied in to the frontier days in Alaska. Across the street and upstairs was The Flame Lounge, the first to feature go-go dancers. The Polaris Lounge was a town bar where you could always find a prostitute or hear a wild story from a bush pilot's life.

Tommy's Elbow Room, my favorite bar escape, was opened in 1946 by Tommy Paskvan, Jr., with money he received from the G.I. Bill. It was a modest-sized bar with a fireplace that covered half of the back wall. Tommy's clientele was a mix of locals and military. It was popular with politicians and government employees. Five or six of us who were friends from Wainwright hung out at Tommy's. That's where we met the owner of a small grocery store who had decided to run for one of the at-large seats in the Alaska House of Representatives. He didn't have a clue about running for office, so three of us who had worked on campaigns at home volunteered to help. He was grateful...until the votes were counted. As I recall there were eighteen running for eight or ten at-large spots. Our guy finished a distant eighteenth. A disappointment, but Tommy's remained a favorite hideout for us. The grocery store owner, however, took his business elsewhere.

In August, the sky started getting dark after dinner, and a new phenomenon appeared nightly. I had no idea what it was the first time I saw it. The night sky was lit by curtains of bright light that appeared to be dancing in the wind. I soon learned that that I was watching the Aurora Borealis or Northern Lights. After dinner, I would choose a grassy spot away from the lights of the buildings and let the Northern Lights entertain me and take my mind off of the turmoil the Army had created during the day.

THIRTY
Ami Has a Plan

Ami and I rarely talked on the phone because long distance calls from Alaska to anywhere were very expensive in 1968, but when she announced in an August letter that she thought it would be a good idea for her to "go ahead and move to Fairbanks," I decided a phone call would be a wise investment.

I had learned from experience that Ami was impulsive, and when she got excited about a new idea, her manic side took the lead and she would make commitments that had not been carefully considered. In short, I needed to know how far out on a limb she had already taken us and what might still be pending.

"In your letter, you said you are 'working on a plan to move to Fairbanks.' So you actually have a plan?" I asked.

"That's it," she replied.

"What's 'it?'" I asked again.

"I *plan* to move to Fairbanks. Of course, you are already there, so it makes sense that you should be the one who finds us a place to live. Maybe there is something available where your friend Arnett and his wife live?"

I was relieved that she had not yet made any drastic commitments like selling the car we would need in Alaska or giving notice on her apartment, but she made it clear that she was determined to be living in Fairbanks "before winter hit," even if it meant flying up with just whatever she could cram into a couple of suitcases.

I suggested that it would be a good idea to have a more detailed plan and she agreed.

Several things needed to happen almost immediately to make her "plan" a reality. First, we needed an affordable place to live. I got lucky, finding a tiny duplex just outside the main gate that I rented virtually sight unseen.

I needed to get to Kansas City ASAP, because there was a lot to accomplish and very little time to do it.

I needed to get a trailer hitch for our Morris Minor, to reserve a small trailer, and to pack it with the most essential household goods and clothes.

Colonel Colonna approved a fourteen-day leave without any hassle, but getting to Kansas City quickly on a commercial flight would have been too expensive for our meager budget, so I started looking for a military flight to anywhere in "the lower 48" that I could ride on for free. I eventually made contact with an operations clerk at Eielson Air Force Base just twenty miles up the road from Fort Wainwright. He informed me that they had an empty cargo plane leaving in about thirty-six hours that he thought I could get on. All he could tell me was that it was going to a U.S. air base, but he did not have a flight plan yet. I figured anywhere in the continental U.S. would be closer to Kansas City than Fairbanks.

"Put me on the list," I said.

A day and a half later at 5:00 a.m., I was standing on the tarmac with five other guys in uniform waiting to board a huge cargo plane. Inside it was eerily empty. The only place for us to sit was on fold down jump seats on both sides of the plane, so we looked like we were lined up to be parachutists.

We started comparing notes about where we thought we were going. There were five different opinions, and each was in a different part of the country.

When they asked for my opinion, I admitted I had no idea, but I hoped the guy who thought we were headed for Tinker Air Force Base outside Oklahoma City was right.

One of our fellow passengers noticed the crew members were carrying some sort of food containers with them when they boarded. We all agreed that was not a good sign. It likely meant it was going to be a long flight, and none of us had thought to bring anything to eat or drink.

When we took off the sound of the engines reverberating off the metal skin of the empty plane drowned out any attempts at conversation, and the noise only got louder as the flight continued. The seats themselves were very uncomfortable, and the cavernous cargo compartment where we were sitting was very cold.

Nobody had thought to bring a book, magazine, or newspaper, so we just sat, staring straight ahead and wondering when it would be over.

Twelve and a half hours after taking off in Alaska, we landed in the dark at an air force base that was virtually shut down for the night. When we got off the plane, we started looking for some indication of where we were. One guy spotted a sign that said "Welcome to Pease Air Force Base."

Nobody in our group had ever heard of Pease Air Force Base, but we noticed a single cab sitting just outside the fence around the airfield.

When the driver spotted us, he came bounding out of his cab, eager to pick up a final fare for the evening.

The driver informed us we were in New Hampshire, about fifty-five miles from Boston's Logan Airport.

"There won't be any more cabs out here tonight, but I'll tell you what I can do," he said. "How many in your group?"

"Six."

"I can get some of your bags in the trunk and I'll tie the rest on top of the cab. If you can all squeeze together, I'll take all of you to Logan for twenty-five dollars each. You can take it or leave it, but if you don't go with me, you will just be standing here with your bags until morning."

"We'll take it," we said.

"Good," he said. "I've been sitting here in the dark in my empty cab for more than an hour, so it will be nice to have someone to talk to for a while."

After the bags were secured, we piled in. The biggest guy sat in the front passenger seat and our smallest sat in his lap. Three were crammed in the back seat and I was stretched out on the floor with six legs draped over me.

"So, where are you guys from?" the driver asked.

When nobody spoke up, he said, "It's not a military secret, is it?"

Our small guy in the front seat finally spoke up.

"We flew in together from Alaska, but I don't know where any of these guys are from. Hell, I don't even know anybody's name."

"How long did you say that flight was?" the driver asked.

"Twelve and a half hours."

We rode the rest of the way in silence.

When we finally arrived at Logan, we must have looked like a clown car in the circus as we tumbled awkwardly out onto the sidewalk.

Once inside, we split up. Finding a flight to Kansas City was at the top of my priority list, so I got in line at the TWA ticket counter.

While I was waiting, I got my pair of "John Lennon glasses" out of my duffel bag and put them on. They were wire frames with round red lenses. They always brightened my mood and made me feel distinctly "unmilitaryish."

I booked a standby fare and headed toward my gate for another long wait. I was in a good mood and didn't notice the two MPs that walked right past me. But they saw me.

MPs are not known for their sense of humor, and these two definitely had their serious faces on.

"Just a minute, soldier. What's with the hippie glasses? You're out of uniform," one of them said.

The last thing I needed was a hassle with a couple of MPs.

"Sergeant, I'm from Fort Wainwright, Alaska," I said, pointing to my unit patch that depicted the Northern Lights over a field of snow. "These glasses are designed especially for operating a vehicle in the snow. For my unit, it's an APC, because we're a mech unit: the 171st Brigade under Colonel O. G. Garrett."

The two MPs just looked at each other. My story may have sounded preposterous to them, but I told it with such sincerity, I thought they might be inclined to believe it. Besides, if they wrote me up for insubordination or being out of uniform, the only thing in it for them was more paperwork.

"Well, it's not snowing in Boston right now," one of the MPs said. "Do you have a pair of non-snow glasses with you?"

"Yes."

"Why don't you put them on for now? Keep those snow glasses in your pocket at least until you get out of the airport."

I simply said, "OK" and we went our separate ways, but as the MPs disappeared into the crowd, I heard one of them say, "Can you believe that bullshit?"

Once I got to Kansas City, I desperately needed sleep, so that's how I spent the rest of my day.

The next morning, our moving-day-push shifted into high gear.

We had reserved a four-foot-by-eight-foot trailer, so we made a four-foot-by-eight-foot rectangle on the apartment floor with masking tape so we could make some decisions about the most important things to take with us before we actually had to start loading the trailer.

Ami informed me that our two adult male cats were definitely on the "essentials" list, so I constructed a bed/carrier for the cats out of heavy corrugate, screen wire, and duct tape. It fit perfectly in the back seat.

When moving day arrived and we hooked up the trailer. It looked huge next to our tiny car. It was hard to tell at first if the car was towing the trailer or if the trailer was pushing the car.

With everything packed, we put the cats in their box and hit the road.

We had gone about four blocks when the cats went berserk: howling, scratching, and totally destroying my corrugate creation. We didn't have time to consider options. I drove straight to a pet store where we bought a sturdy wooden carrier. The next stop was the vet's office for some cat tranquilizers.

The tranquilizers kept the cats quiet and sleeping all day, but when we stopped for the night, they were wide awake and wanted to play.

We made it to Fargo on that first short day and spent the night in a city park. Ami slept in the car and I slept on a picnic table.

Over the next couple of days, we made up the lost time and when we hit the Alaska Highway in Dawson Creek, we were back on schedule.

The whole trip was an adventure—beautiful scenery, plentiful wildlife—and every night we found a little family-run inn to stay. Most of our breakfasts and dinners on the Alaska Highway were served at communal tables where we exchanged information about the road ahead with those going the other direction.

The Canadian portion of the Highway was not paved, so at times, the road suddenly became rough and unpredictable. At dinner the night before our last day on the road, we had been in our car for a week and were anxious to get to get to our new home. Our fellow diners that night assured us that the last fifty miles of unpaved highway were no different than the previous thousand, and once we were back on the blacktop, it would be smooth sailing to Fairbanks.

All signs pointed to an uneventful day, but the Highway had a final surprise for us. At Haines Junction, the road splits. The Alaska Highway makes a sharp right, heading west toward Fairbanks. As I turned, I drove over a large rock with such force that it snapped the four bolts holding the right front wheel in place.

I got out to survey the damage and see if there was any possibility that I could figure out a makeshift repair that would allow us to limp a couple of hundred miles to Fairbanks. That's when I realized that I had picked the best possible place to break down. We were right in front of the only gas station and auto repair shop within fifty miles.

The owner/mechanic surveyed the damage, decided he could probably figure out a way to fix it, but he would have to charge me twenty-five US dollars.

"You'll have to leave the car with me for a while, he said. "And it may take a couple of hours."

I assured him that arrangement would be fine with us.

He suggested we go across the road to the restaurant/bar/inn where we could get something to eat and wait with our sleeping cats in relative comfort.

So, we picked up the cat carrier, crossed the Highway, and walked into the bar.

That's when the floor show began.

Three of the bar patrons had brought their dogs with them. All three were big dogs. But two of them were mellow, laid-back creatures who didn't care who or what came into the bar.

The third, however, wasn't really a dog. He was a young wolf whose owner was trying to raise as a pet. The wolf was going to defend his turf against all enemies foreign or domesticated. And that meant attacking whatever was in that wooden box and whoever was holding it (that would be me.).

The noise woke up the other two dogs and they joined the melee.

The bartender and the owner of the wolf pulled the beast out of the mess, and the owner was told to take his wild animal outside. More complaints ensued.

"He's not a wild animal and besides, we were here first," the owner said.

The bartender served the wolf's owner a beer on the house and order was restored. He took our food order, and we were able to eat a peaceful lunch.

After lunch, I went across the street to check on progress with the repairs. It didn't look like there had been any, but the mechanic assured me that he would get it fixed.

Ami and I decided that we would spend the night there, and we got one of the inn's rooms. It was directly over the bar, and even without the dogs, it was noisy all night long.

In the morning, we had a note from the mechanic informing us that our car was ready, but he wouldn't be back for a while. He had gone to help a Mountie tag a bear.

When he returned, he said our car took much longer than he expected (I figured he had spent at least eight hours working on it) and he apologized, but asked if I could pay him a little more. I gritted my teeth and mumbled "How much?"

"Could you make it thirty-five dollars?" he said.

I gave him thirty-five dollars without complaint.

"Oh, one other thing," he said. "I had to use a torch to cut a hole in the floor so I could reach behind the broken mounting and put in new bolts. The torch kind of caught your carpet on fire. I patched the hole and the floor mat covers the burned carpet, but it probably won't smell very good for a few days."

We thanked him for the effort, put the cats back in the car, and headed for Fairbanks.

The repaired mechanism worked perfectly.

It had just started to snow when we arrived in Fairbanks on a late September afternoon. We found our duplex easily, but it was a bit of a shock. It was more rundown than I remembered, and it was still showing the after-effects from last year's flood outside, but we felt better when we got everything unloaded.

We got a foot of snow overnight, but it was comforting to learn that the apartment would keep us warm.

THIRTY-ONE

Settling Down in Fairbanks Town

My life changed dramatically once Ami and I were living together as a couple off the base.

For one thing, our duplex replaced the bars on Second Avenue as the place for my small circle of friends to hang out. John Polodna was probably the most frequent and most welcome guest because he never came empty-handed. We were never surprised when we answered a knock on the door and found a familiar face who just happened to be in the neighborhood with a couple of six packs or a bottle of wine.

Money—or the lack of it—was a constant concern. Ami received a monthly housing allowance check from the Army, and after moving to Fairbanks, it was increased to partially offset the high cost of living in Alaska. That was our only steady, predictable income.

Ami took me to work in the morning so she could use the car to look for a job. I don't know if the Fairbanks businesses were not interested in someone with her work history or if she wasn't interested in any of them, but the bottom line was she never got a job.

When I found out that every office in the battalion sent someone out for donuts every morning, I decided to establish a donut
delivery service. Each group had to have a standing order and someone designated to pay me every day. Instead of purchasing whatever
the commissary had to offer—which sometimes included yesterday's
leftovers—I purchased my donuts fresh and warm from a bakery in
town. They were a major improvement from the donuts they had
been getting from the commissary. I charged a nickel more per donut
for my delivery service and no one complained about the price. In
fact, a couple of other offices heard about my service and signed on.
It did not generate a lot of income, but every little bit helped. It also
enabled me to make connections with all the company clerks—the
"Radar O'Reilly's" of the Army who always knew what was really
going on.

Ami began to get interested in this little business and made
many of the deliveries. She suggested we expand the product offering
to include "the sweet roll of the day." She would bake them in our
tiny kitchen. We could charge more and keep all the profit.

Her first offering was Orange Rolls. They were a huge hit, and
we were soon selling more rolls than donuts.

I thought she would soon get tired or bored of the daily routine
and want to quit, but she didn't. Perhaps it was the chance to be her
own boss or the opportunity to experiment whenever she wanted
to. But for whatever reason, she stuck with it.

Polodna introduced us to Dick Pohorsky and his wife who lived
just a block and a half from us and became our only "couple friends."
Dick and I discovered a truly Alaskan business opportunity that was

hard work, potentially lucrative, sometimes fun, and occasionally dangerous.

In Alaska, snow is more than a temporary annoyance. The snow that falls in October will still be there six months later. It just keeps piling up. The weight of the winter's accumulated snow can become a problem for some homeowners. If the pitch of the roof is not steep enough, the roof can collapse. However, a more common problem is the formation of ice dams in the gutters. As the snow next to the roof melts, the water is trapped and seeps under the shingles and eventually leaks through the ceiling. Often it fills ceiling light fixtures and can cause electrical shorts or even fires.

When I discovered the ceiling light in our bathroom was full of water, something had to be done.

The solution was to shovel the snow off the roof. I recruited Dick to help me. We were nearly finished when I lost my footing and slid about twenty feet down the roof and went flying through the air. For a split second I was in a total panic, but then I landed in a three-foot deep snowdrift that we had created with the snow we had shoveled off the roof. Dick was concerned and tried to see what had happened to me, but he lost his balance as well and ended up in the snow beside me. We lay there laughing uncontrollably, then got up, and did it again on purpose—about a dozen times. We had invented a new sport as well as a new business. From then on, we celebrated the end of each roof-shoveling job with a few rounds of freestyle roof jumping.

Another budget stretcher was free food. When we returned from maneuvers, there often were a few cases of C-rations left. Rather than store them for an unknown period of time, the Supply Officer gave them out to anyone who was interested. I made it a point to always be near the front of the line. C-rations were not fine dining, but Ami was a good and creative cook. With a little imagination and appropriate spices, she was able to turn the most mundane C-rations into a tasty meal.

Our neighbors in the other half of the duplex turned out to be an unexpected source of freebies. They were truck drivers who delivered food and supplies from the post's central warehouse to all the mess halls. Occasionally, one of them would knock on our door and offer us a roast or some other big hunk of meat.

"We had this left over today and thought you might be able to use it," they would say.

We also became skilled at finding free events or other entertainment: native dance exhibitions, local snowmobile and dog-sled races, and the annual Nenana Ice Classic.

The Ice Classic is a uniquely Alaskan event held in early February in the village of Nenana on the banks of the Tanana River. This day-long event is the kick-off for ticket sales to individuals who want to try to predict the exact time the ice on the river at Nenana will break up. Only residents of Alaska and the Yukon and Northwest Territories in Canada can purchase a ticket registering their guess. The person or persons who pick the exact time wins the proceeds from the ticket sales. As I recall, the jackpot was about $250,000 at that time.

The event itself draws a crowd to watch as a large tripod is set up in the middle of the frozen river and is connected to the official timer on the riverbank. Other activities during the day include dog sled races, a parka parade (an opportunity for native women to display their elaborately decorated handmade parkas), and a community dinner featuring traditional native food.

Our day in Nenana was a memorable one, but getting there was memorable for another reason. There were five of us who wanted to make the trip, but only one had a vehicle big enough for all of us: a VW minibus. As we got ready to leave Fairbanks, I tossed my snow shovel in the back "just in case." The others gave me a hard time for being such a worrier, but I just repeated one of my grandmother's favorite warnings: "Better safe than sorry."

The only way to get to Nenana was an "ice road." It's a dirt road in the summer, but it's not plowed in the winter, so the traffic compresses the snow until it becomes a solid sheet of ice.

As we came around a curve, the minibus lost what little traction it had, and it spun around and went tail end first into eighteen-inch-deep snow on the side of the road. We got out of the VW, and I tried not to gloat as I retrieved our one shovel. With just one shovel, we had several hours of work ahead of us. But a few minutes later, another car stopped. The driver pulled a shovel out of his trunk and, without saying a word, began shoveling. In half an hour, we had six shovelers and had cleared a path up the embankment to the road.

The next vehicle to stop was a big pickup. The driver jumped out, crawled under his truck, and fastened chains to the rear tires and connected the two vehicles with a length of chain. Four or five guys climbed into the back of the pickup to put more weight on the back wheels. Everyone else pushed.

The VW rolled easily back up onto the road.

A cheer and a round of high fives followed. One by one, everybody resumed their journeys. The truck driver who had to remove his chains was the last to go.

"That was amazing," I said. "I think everyone who came down the road stopped and helped."

"That was great teamwork," the truck driver said. "But there was nothing amazing about it. It's Alaska. You never pass someone in trouble on the road because you don't know when the next car will come by, and in this weather, you could die. You always stop. It's just what you do."

THIRTY-TWO

The Waiting Game

I had only been in Alaska for about six weeks when I submitted my written request for reclassification and release from the Army to my company commander, Lt. John Zarro. The document combined my written responses to questions about my background and my religious beliefs, letters of support I had received, and interviews conducted in Alaska with an Army chaplain, a psychiatrist, and an investigating officer. At that point, it was about forty pages long.

As the first link in the chain of command, Lt. Zarro's role was to review my request, recommend it be approved or denied, and send it up to the next level. Eventually, it would end up in the office of Major General Kenneth Wichman in the Pentagon. As Adjutant General, U.S. Army, he had the ultimate authority to make decisions on personnel issues. However, once my paperwork left my hands, it seemed to disappear. Nobody knew where it was on any given day or how many others were still on the list to review it before a decision was made.

It was July, but the thought had already occurred to me that if my request was approved, I might choose to stay in Alaska permanently. Of course, that was a pretty big *if* because more than eighty-five percent of the requests like mine were denied.

To get more information about the decision-making process, I met with Sgt. Graves, the battalion's "go-to guy." He always knew what was happening anywhere on the base, how to cut through the red tape to get things done, who you could count on, and who was just blowing smoke.

I asked him how long he thought it would take to get an answer.

"I don't even know who will make that decision," he said, "but if I were you, I would count on waiting months rather than weeks."

"Why will it take so long?" I asked.

He laughed.

"A private in Alaska who says he's a conscientious objector is not someone who is likely to move up quickly on anyone's priority list."

Of course, he was right. The weeks piled up slowly, and my anxiety grew along with it. I had invested a lot of time and effort compiling that document. It represented my past, present, and future. Couldn't someone recognize that and expedite their decision?

The wait was frustrating, but during that time, I realized I should be grateful to Captain Douglas at Fort Dix for failing to follow proper procedure and for falsifying my training records. If he had followed regulations, my request almost certainly would have been denied immediately. I would have been court-martialed, spent time in the stockade, and ultimately been given a dishonorable discharge.

At Fort Dix, I was in Basic Training, so when I said I was a conscientious objector, no one believed I was sincere. They assumed I was just trying to stay out of Vietnam.

Once I was at Fort Wainwright, however, Vietnam was not an issue. Everyone knew that an enlisted man or draftee who was not interested in a military career would almost always get an "early out," and finish his military service in Fairbanks a month or more before scheduled.

At Wainwright, I figured that if my request was denied, Colonel Colonna might have me continue in my present job. There was always a chance that I would be moved to a line company where I would be expected to use a weapon.

If my request was approved, I could return to a good job at Hallmark or stay in Fairbanks.

Ami and I discussed all these options at length, but we didn't come up with the same answer every time. When she first got to Fairbanks, staying put was our first choice.

Then winter came roaring in. The old-timers were right: the winter of 1968–1969 was especially brutal.

The low temperature at Fairbanks International Airport that winter was −61°, the lowest since the airport was constructed in 1949, and it has not been equaled since. The average high for the month of January was −19°, and for thirty-two straight days, the low temperature was −40° or below.

There was little if anything I could do about the winter except endure it as I waited to hear from the unknown people who were going to make a decision that would change my life again.

And even though there was still a foot of snow on the ground when I turned the calendar page to January 1969, the smart money was betting that Spring would arrive before the Army bureaucrats could make a decision.

THIRTY-THREE
The Verdict

The rumors started midmorning on another cold winter day when Colonel Garrett, the brigade commander and Lt. Col. Colonna's boss, showed up unexpectedly and went into Colonna's office with a Captain from the AG's office. The speculation was that an unannounced field exercise was in the works because the new USARAL Commanding General wanted to test the post's overall readiness.

When they left, Lt. Magnificci came to see me and find out what I had heard.

"Nothing," I said.

"Come on," he prodded. "Something is going on."

I thought for a moment. Except for a large photo on the front page of the *News-Miner* that showed about two dozen people lined up outside the Dairy Queen and a smaller inset picture of the Key Bank's time and temperature sign indicating the temperature was –21°, I could not think of anything remarkable that I had heard about in the last twenty-four hours.

"Well, the Dairy Queen reopened," I said. That was actually pretty big news in Fairbanks. The owners closed down and went

South for a couple of months in the winter. When they reopened, it was considered a sign of Spring on par with the first crocus or the first robin in the lower forty-eight. After the harsh winter that was still hanging on, any sign of Spring was welcome.

Magnificci just scoffed.

"We're going out to the boonies, aren't we?" he said.

"Too cold," was my only answer.

Magnificci had already made up his mind and kept pushing for something that wasn't there.

"You were here in December or have you forgotten," he said.

Yes, we had gone on maneuvers in December when the temperature was hovering around 0°. We pitched our tents in the snow. There were a lot of complaints about the weather and a hopeful rumor that the exercise would be cut short had circulated.

But Lt. Col. Colonna was not a fair-weather soldier. He got on the radio and delivered a challenge to his officers.

"This is Grey Fox Leader," he said bluntly. "I know there has been some talk about cutting this exercise short. That is not going to happen. I want you to always remember that lesser dogs may turn and run, but the Grey Fox always stands his ground."

We stayed to the end and then, as if to put an exclamation point on it, Colonel Colonna sat on top of the APC and rode all the way back to the base in the cold, while the rest of us huddled inside.

"Sure. I remember December, but this is different," I said.

Even though the average daily temperature for the past month had been −19°, Magnificci still wasn't buying it.

After lunch, Sgt. Graves knocked on my door. "The Colonel wants to see us," he said. The sergeant followed me across the hall where Lt. Col. Colonna was waiting for us.

"Have a seat," he said as he removed a single sheet of paper from the file folder on his desk and slid it toward me.

"I have some mail for you," he said.

It appeared to be a makeshift form that had been mimeographed on a sheet of Department of the Army letterhead. It was addressed to "Commanding General, U.S. Army, Alaska," but I knew immediately what it was about.

The decision I had been waiting for since July It was the verdict.

THE VERDICT

DEPARTMENT OF THE ARMY
OFFICE OF THE ADJUTANT GENERAL
WASHINGTON, D.C. 20315

AGPO-SS Parkinson, Jan L.   19 February 1969
RA 16962677 (26 Jul 68)

SUBJECT: Separation

Commanding General
U. S. Army, Alaska
ATTN: ARAAG-PA
APO Seattle 98749

1. Reference your Omt 11 dated 22 January 1969 regarding the separation
of PVT Jan L. Parkinson, RA 16962677, HHC, 1st Bn, 47th Inf, APO Seattle
98731.
2. Separation /x/ approved, PNMO. /_/ disapproved.

3. Authority:

    /_/ Section II, Chap 5, AR 635-200, SPN 21L

    /_/ Section IV, Chap 5, AR 635-200, SPN 314

    /_/ Section VIII, Chap 5, AR 635-200, SPN 41C

    /_/ Section VIII, Chap 5, AR 635-200, SPN 413

    /_/ Section IX, Chap 5, AR 635-200, SPN 414

    /x/ AR 635-20, SPN 318

4. Comments:

BY ORDER OF THE SECRETARY OF THE ARMY:

Adjutant General
ALICE I. HAMPSON, MAJ, AGC
Sep & Ret Affairs Div, TAGO

File M
AGPERSCEN (AG-6010)
19 Feb 69
Date   Clerk
A GPO: 1968-324-176

PERMANENT

AGPZ FL 13, 1 Oct 68

159

"You know what this is, don't you?" he asked.

"Yes, sir."

"I expect the next few days will be busy with paperwork, turning in your gear and just dealing with the bureaucracy to wrap this up so you can get home or wherever you plan to go. I suggest you seek Sgt. Graves' guidance, because…

He paused and, for the first time since I'd met him, he grinned.

"Because I don't have any experience in trying to get out of the Army."

Sgt. Graves and I exchanged a quick look of surprise: The Colonel had just made a joke!

But the serious Colonel quickly returned.

"I suppose you and your wife and some of your friends will want to celebrate, but I would appreciate it if you would keep your celebrating away from the battalion area."

I assured him that would not be a problem, but his comment puzzled me, because I had never thought of this as a competition.

Sgt. Graves provided all the necessary forms, a separation checklist, and his idea of humor: a reenlistment brochure.

The first item on the checklist was "Report to Personnel Building 155 ASAP."

I had only been to the Personnel Building once before. It was my very first day in Fairbanks, and it's where I took my paperwork to be officially "in-processed." Now, I would be returning to be "out-processed," bringing everything full circle.

The personnel clerk who was assigned to help me offered a few disclaimers.

"Most of the men who complete their service obligation in Alaska let the Army fly them to their permanent home of record and are out-processed there. They avoid a lot of the red tape," he said. "Most of them are single or have a spouse waiting for them there. I tell you that because I have never handled a conscientious objector discharge before."

"I understand," I said. "I appreciate your help. I'm sure we will be fine."

And we were.

The clerk was smart, thorough, and careful. We moved through the required forms quickly with just one pause.

"The last question is 'Type of Discharge.' Who tells me what to put there?" he asked.

"Nobody," I said. "The regulation doesn't designate anyone in particular, and you are only required to include an explanation if you choose 'Dishonorable.' So, you choose."

"You're kidding," he said.

"No, I'm not. The generals and colonels had their chance, and I doubt that they thought about their answer as carefully as you already have. It's your call," I said.

He smiled broadly and, with a dramatic flourish, typed an "X" in the box next to "Honorable."

"Thank you," he said. "Every day I sit at this desk and shuffle paper. Today I feel like I've done something productive. That by itself is worthy of 'Honorable.'"

THIRTY-FOUR

The Tipping Point

I t was a mystery to me: why it would take 224 days—more than seven months—to review and ultimately approve my petition to be reclassified as a noncombatant and released from the Army.

The process began when I submitted the document to Lt. Zarro, my company commander, who reviewed it, recommended approval, and passed it on up the chain of command. My documents landed on the desk of Maj. Gen. Wickham in Washington D.C. in late September. Given the importance the Army attaches to the chain of command concept, I assumed that Wickham would base his decision largely on those evaluations.

He did not.

Instead, he went outside the command structure of the Army, and on October 22, he wrote to Lewis B. Hershey, the head of the Selective Service System and asked him for an answer to a hypothetical situation: if a man brought this claim to a draft board under his jurisdiction, what would his response be?

A week later, Hershey replied that this hypothetical person would be classified I-0, a conscientious objector. But when Wickham received the reply to his inquiry from the head of the Selective Service System, he did nothing with it for nearly two months. On December 26, 1968, he sent the entire file back to Alaska with a six-word cover memo: "Returned for compliance with Paragraph 4d."

When Lt. Col. Colonna responded a few days later, he attached the report of an interview I had with Brigade Chaplain Robert Ennis that said in part:

> *This interview was made to comply with Army regulation 635-20 paragraph 4(d). My qualification to conduct this interview is based on experience while assigned to Fort Knox, Kentucky, my last duty station.*
>
> *Specialist 4 Parkinson presented the most well-constructed argument for conscientious objection that I have ever heard. In no sense is he an extremist and unrealistic idealist, but rather a very sincere man who cannot conform the goals of the Army with the dictates of his conscience. I recommend that this man be released from the Army on the basis of verified grounds for conscientious objection.*
>
> *Chaplain Robert J. Ennis*

Was Chaplain Ennis' letter the tipping point?

There's no way we could ever know for sure, but I do know that shortly after the letter was sent to Washington, Maj. Gen. Wickham's office distributed the news that my request was approved.

EPILOGUE

I n January 2013, I wrote to the National Personnel Records Center in St. Louis, Missouri, and requested a copy of my military records from the 408 days I spent in the U.S. Army in 1968 and 1969. Most of the items in my file were related to my effort to be reclassified as a conscientious objector.

As I read through the fifty-plus pages of documents, memos, and letters, I was surprised at how many details easily came back to me. Even more unexpected was the way the emotions I felt at the time returned fresh, as if being lived for the first time.

I am seventy-seven years old now, so 408 days does not sound like such a long time, but when Ami and I had been waiting—more or less patiently—for the Army to make up its collective mind, it seemed like a lifetime. When they finally did issue their verdict, it felt more like an eviction notice. The Army wanted me out of there as soon as possible.

Staying in Fairbanks was still an option, but I would need a job immediately. As I was searching for employment, I discovered an interesting trait shared by many people who settle in Alaska: where they live is more important to them than what they do for a living. A civilian neighbor in Fairbanks was a good example. He had a PhD in Biology, but when he moved North, the only job that he could find was driving a truck for a lumber yard.

I knew that would not be a good model for me. I could not spend eight to ten hours a day at a job that didn't have its own built-in satisfactions just to have an opportunity to walk in the woods on the weekends.

So, I made a list of all the companies that might use a writer, an advertising creative, or a marketing person. Although the town had two daily papers—the *Fairbanks News-Miner* and *Jessen's Daily*—neither was hiring reporters, editors, or even ad sales reps. The retailers and other businesses of any size were part of chains, and their advertising and marketing functions were managed in larger markets.

If we returned to Kansas City, Hallmark would have a job with a decent salary and benefits. And as a creative company, there were creative opportunities as well. That made our decision easier: We returned "home" and even found an apartment in our old neighborhood.

Two weeks after I started back at Hallmark, I got a call from the editor of *Jessen's Daily* offering me a job as a reporter. I was disappointed that I had to turn him down, and for several months, I thought about what might have been. However, before the end of the year, *Jessen's Daily* announced they were closing the paper.

My Hallmark career was a better story. I spent nearly forty-four years at Hallmark, before retiring in 2010 as Vice President of Hallmark Hall of Fame Productions. We made three or four feature-length movies a year for broadcast on the Hallmark Hall of Fame on CBS. I had the best job in America.

Soon after we returned to Kansas City, we learned that Ami was pregnant. We were both very excited and spent many hours fixing up the sunroom at the back of our apartment as a nursery.

Our daughter Kirsten was born in November 1969. She was a healthy and happy baby. Initially, Ami was enjoying being a mom.

Our world was looking pretty good.

However, there was one storm cloud on the horizon: because I was released early from the Army, I had to notify my draft board that I was available for alternative service to fulfill my service obligation. To my surprise, the draft board said "no thanks." The Army had taken so long to act on my request, there were only a few months left on my service obligation, and the draft board knew that no organization would be interested in training someone who would be available for such a short time.

Ami's initial enthusiasm for full-time motherhood began to wane. One day in the early Fall 1971, she called me at work and suggested we go out to dinner.

She arranged for a sitter and even bought a new dress for the occasion. It was a pleasant night out until the waiter brought the check. That's when she announced that she had seen an attorney and was filing for divorce.

I was stunned, but she had "worked it all out," including picking the date for me to move out. She also had enrolled Kirsten in a Montessori preschool. Ami would keep Kirsten during the week, and I would pick her up after school on Friday and take her back to Ami on Sunday night.

On one of those weekends, she phoned me on Sunday and said she was on the beach in San Diego and wasn't coming back. I could keep her furniture, her LPs, her cats, her aquarium, and, oh yeah, our daughter. Ami got her freedom.

I got the better part of that deal.

A couple of months later, I got full legal custody. Ami moved back to KC once for a short period, but she has moved more times than I could count. Kirsten has seen her briefly only a few times since she was four.

As I began to write my story, I kept coming back to a single question: Whatever happened to Lieutenant Colonel Gary S. Colonna?

I really did not know anything of significance about him. He seemed to be much older than me, so I wondered if he was even still living.

So, I turned to Google for answers.

I not only found him but also discovered he lives in Lansing, Kansas, just twenty-two miles from my house. He had retired from the Army, and since Lansing borders on the south edge of Leavenworth, I guessed that his last assignment was at the Army Staff and Command College at Fort Leavenworth.

I decided to write to him. It was just a short note asking if he remembered me and thanking him for his support, his integrity, compassion, and high ethical standards.

I was pleased to get a short hand-written note in response. He said, "Of course, I remember you." He ended his reply by saying "I think we both tried our best to act in a manner that was consistent with our beliefs and in the best interests of our country. And I feel we both succeeded."

ACKNOWLEDGMENTS

W hen people ask me about this book, they usually refer to it as "your book" and because the work of putting actual words on paper occurred while I was alone in a room with my computer, I am reasonably comfortable referring to it as "my book." But as anyone who has ever attempted write a book knows, a lot of people contribute to the process and I want them all to know how much I appreciate their contributions.

A special thanks to Rev. Tom Hayes of the Episcopal Peace Fellowship who opened the first door and offered information and wise counsel throughout the process. My sincere appreciation for all the people who wrote letters of support that became a major part of this effort: Rev. Allen Hingston, Chaplain Edward A. Sterling, Rev. William T. Warren, Chaplain Clyde J. Wood, Chaplain Robert J. Ennis, Lt. Col. Gary Colonna, James E. Brown, Dr. Gordon Grundy, David A. Mead, Almond (Ami) Parkinson, Betty Parkinson, John B. Olmsted, Captain Michael Romney, and Richard W. Willhardt.

When the MLA Style Guide, the Associated Press Stylebook, the Chicago Manual of Style, and the DOD Military Writing Style Book couldn't agree about grammar, punctuation, and even spelling, my daughter, Kirsten Parkinson, was my guide out of the English language wilderness.

To Melinda Worth Popham who knows a thing or two about writing my sincere thanks for sharing her insights, talent, and time with someone trying to become a writer worthy of her confidence.

Thanks to Jayne Quimby for her support, suggestions, encouragement. and for reading every draft (and there were many) without losing her enthusiasm for the story.

And sincere gratitude to Joan Gilson and the Writers' Group at Colonial UCC Church in Prairie Village, Kansas for being my patient readers, listeners and cheerleaders.